L'art de la
LISTE

By the same author

L'art de la
SIMPLICITÉ

L'art de la
LISTE

SIMPLIFY
ORGANISE
ENRICH YOUR LIFE

Dominique Loreau

TRAPEZE

This edition first published in Great Britain in 2018 by Trapeze,
an imprint of The Orion Publishing Group Ltd
Carmelite House, 50 Victoria Embankment,
London EC4Y 0DZ

An Hachette UK company

3 5 7 9 10 8 6 4

A CIP catalogue record for this book is
available from the British Library.

ISBN (Hardback): 978 1 409 18291 7
ISBN (eBook): 978 1 409 18293 1

Typeset by carrdesignstudio.com

Printed in Great Britain by CPI Group (UK) Ltd, Croydon CR0 4YY

MIX
Paper from
responsible sources
FSC
www.fsc.org   FSC® C104740

Contents

This book is for anyone who wants to:

Simplify their life

Discover themselves

Keep their best memories

Discover 1,001 small pleasures

Find their true path in life.

'On my desk my notebook
Still blank
The three days of the year.'

Haiku by Yoshida Nobuko

Introduction

'There are more things in heaven and earth, Horatio, than are dreamt of in your philosophy.'

William Shakespeare

Lists of:

Funny things

Things which make the heart beat faster

Extremely tiresome things

Pleasant things

And, under the last heading:

'It is very pleasant, on a cold winter's night, to be buried with
your lover under a heap of quilts'

Or:

'To go to bed alone in a room which smells just perfect.'

This is the system Sei Shonagon – the most famous courtesan to sixteenth-century Japanese writers – used to record what she experienced in the course of her life.

From hieroglyphs to anthologies, miscellanies, almanacs,

compendiums and encyclopedias, humankind has always felt the need to write or draw ideas, events and facts, and to present these in detailed and methodical lists. And whether these lists are presented on stone, bark, clay, paper or computer screens, the impulse remains the same.

In monasteries in the Middle Ages, the first books were written in the form of lists. In Asia, emperors ordered clerks to survey the population and make inventories of all kinds of things: medicinal plants, fauna, local customs, culinary specialities, religious cults…

What these people shared was a desire for universal knowledge and, through that, self-knowledge. Thanks to these enumerations, these lists, humankind could discover the universe, seize the essence of it, and understand it better.

Humanity continues to pursue this quest for knowledge: what is our true nature, what is the meaning of life?

By virtue of its concise, contained form, the simplicity of its presentation and the immediacy of its approach, the list gives us an entry point into a potentially unlimited exploration of our lives. A form of language and of knowledge, the list allows us to approach facts with a magical clarity that reveals their true meaning.

Lists allow you to explore your memories, your dreams and your preferences. They allow you to look deep inside yourself, and find all sorts of hidden treasures: creative powers, abandoned dreams, parts of yourself you had pushed away or ignored, forgotten memories. They allow you to reorder yourself, to reflect, to evolve, to tame silence and solitude, to simplify life and give it more value. And what could be more gratifying or more effective than doing something by yourself and for yourself?

Because we are short of time, we often forget who we are. The elliptical form of the list is perfect for our day and age, not only because it gives us the opportunity to reach self-awareness, but also because it gives us the possibility of spiritual renewal.

It goes without saying that lists allow us to clarify our thoughts and take the weight off our minds. Zen philosophy counsels us to abide by forms in order to liberate ourselves from them and achieve freedom. Lists are that form. They will give you more lucidity and more ease in everyday life; they will hugely enrich every sphere of your life.

Why write lists?

*'Why are clouds so beautiful? If I tried to list the reasons,
I would need more than one page. They are beautiful
when they are useful and wished for, but also when
they are threatening. When they are white like sheep
or black like wolves.'*

Jean-Luc Nothias, *Le Figaro,* 17 August 2005

We may not be aware of this, but our very being is a collection of lists. Everything must belong to the past, the present or the future.

Lists belong not only in everyday life, but also in the life of the mind. They are an indispensable crutch. We draft hundreds of them: lists of what we have to do, would like to do, have done, lists of addresses, recipes, books we have read, things to take on holiday, plans… They help us to 'function'.

We don't keep or archive our lists; we don't give them the recognition they deserve. And yet they help us so much: to keep control of our lives, to save time, to avoid confusion, stress and forgetting… So why don't we accept, once and for all, that lists are necessary, useful and precious. And that, by learning how to organise them, to love them and to use them intelligently, we can live more simply, more easily and more intensely.

Personal development

In the past, we had priests, masters and elders. We could trust these people, and ask them for practical, moral or spiritual advice. Today, they have been replaced by therapists, by various techniques of 'personal development', by psychologists, psychotherapists, life coaches and, of course, the pharmaceutical industry. But that doesn't make personal development any less important: it is the basis of everything. Self-help books continue to flood the market-place, offering methods and techniques to help you become your best possible self. And all, in some way, recommend taking notes and making lists.

Many different voices are vying for our attention – and we may be interested in many of them – but we cannot gain a deep under-standing of all these techniques. We hope that the next magazine we buy, the next book we read, will offer us a better, easier, quicker approach… So we plough on with our reading, tirelessly striving to find the latest 'secret' miracle for losing weight or de-stressing, for finding happiness or our very own Prince Charming.

But, if we are honest with ourselves, what do we achieve by doing this? Do we actually put any of it into practice? At the end of the day, what do we really get from all the money and time we invest?

The reason we read these books is because we want to change and evolve. But to do that we need to act, to throw ourselves into our plans. Merely reading advice will not produce results. It's what we do with the advice that matters.

So if you really want to take advantage of the advice you read, buy a nice, big notebook and write it all down. Write down all the recommended topics for 'To Do' lists, the exercises which strike you as effective and which suit your personality; focus on certain points of interest. With a notebook to hand, you will know where to write the things you want to try and to develop. You will write your own advice on the things which have meaning and importance to you.

You will also know where to write the small things which you would like to remember, the things you often want to write down, perhaps without even knowing why, but never do. Why don't we write these things down? Firstly, out of laziness or a vague feeling of 'what's the point?' But the key problem is disorganisation. A little voice in you whines: 'But where will I write that down? That piece of paper's just going to end up in the bin or under the sofa…' And so you shelve the idea, knowing that these 'notes to self' will simply disappear. But, as this book will show you, making lists is neither a vanity nor a chore. It is not just something for the scatterbrained among us. On the contrary, making systems is a way to make meaning, to back up your memory, to refresh it, and to live in a more intense way.

A question of personality

'Lists? Oh, I'm always making lists. I couldn't live without them. They comfort me.'

'Lists? I have them on the go all the time. They're my main point of reference, my support.'

'Lists? I always leave them on the table. But at least they remind me what to put in my bag.'

When I ask my friends whether they make lists, some become distant, almost condescending, and reply that yes, of course they do, they make shopping lists. But apart from that, why bother? Other friends light up: 'Yes, of course, I make lists of everything, absolutely everything: places I'd like to visit, my possessions, the presents I have to buy that year.'

Perhaps this strikes you as an odd question. But the answers are instructive.

'Lists? My father wrote the most wonderful lists. He had a very particular way of writing them, sometimes for that day, sometimes for that week, sometimes for that year. He used to fold them up in concertinas. I would have liked to keep some, they were unique.'

'I make a list of all the plants and trees we have in our garden.'

Apart from the fact that people who make lists generally like to talk about them a lot, the subject of lists can reveal a new side to someone's personality. We may discover that a person we thought hadn't any particular passions is in fact an artist; that someone we saw as a bohemian keeps track of their finances down to the last penny.

A person's relationship with lists says a lot about their temperament, and people who write them tend to be very interesting, in the same way collectors are. There is even a website (www.echolaliste. com) for people who want to publish their lists. At the time of writing, 2,000 lists had been published.

But lists are also a cultural phenomenon. A student at Todai, the most prestigious university in Japan, said that he and his friends had been taught to write everything down: the films they'd watched, the books they'd read or had to read, the exhibitions and baseball games they'd attended, the places they'd visited… That way, come exam time, they would have a wide range of knowledge at their fingertips, gleaned from very different contexts.

In Japan, people often talk about listomania. The Japanese like perfection, they like extremes. That is part of the national character. Some are methodical to a degree unimaginable to people of other nationalities; they list everything and want to take full possession of what they know. How can we explain this phenomenon? It comes down to the love of possessing knowledge, and keeping the traces of your life, without cluttering it with material things (brochures, cinema tickets, newspaper articles, and so on); the art of possessing without possessing, of having everything by having nothing. Is this because Zen philosophy advises us to get rid of useless things in order to devote ourselves to life?

Making lists is a way of savouring life; it is also a way of stretching time, of punctuating it, measuring it and collecting its precious moments.

The art of little: style without syntax

Dawn
The breath of whales
A frozen sea.

Gyodai

The list is the most concise form of expression available to us. But, paradoxically, its elliptical nature allows us to be as exhaustive as possible. Its brevity leads us to the truth of things. And it can often do that far more powerfully than phrases weighed down by syntax. Writing lists teaches us to reduce the number of words and phrases we use; to employ short, succinct formulations that are easy to write, read, reread and understand; to achieve maximum meaning in minimum words. Perhaps, then, we can even find a moment of pure poetry, a diamond in the rough. Lists can become art forms, like haikus.

Poetic expression has always been a part of writing. So why is it not part of making lists? The Japanese often express themselves in haikus. These poems are a sort of visualisation, and they should, in principle, never exceed the length of a breath. But our Western civilisation suffers from long-windedness. We are intoxicated by phrases and long expositions. We lose ourselves in wasted words, words which contain no meaning or depth. Our minds become encumbered by the number of words we use, and the length of those words.

Words, words and more words. In the same way that weeds stunt

9

the growth of plants, this waffle stunts our thoughts. The haiku, on the other hand, is so concise and so dense that its meaning surges forth like a flame, immediately taking us to the heart of things.

The power of the haiku lies in its simple juxtaposition of words, its lack of linear logic. As the eminent Japanese-to-French translator Corinne Atlan explains, the haiku doesn't worship at the feet of Cartesian logic. Without even 'expressing' anything, the very juxtaposition of certain phrases can spark a surprise connection, and allow us to seize what 'constructed' language does not allow us to express.

Lists are sequences of words. They allow us to condense our experience in a profound, poetic way, to seize the essence of a moment. With a list, there is no verbal fog to conceal what we are trying to express. Don't maxims and proverbs follow the same principle?

Writing, correcting, editing, clarifying, refining... the work of deleting, of filtering, of gradually trimming back the superfluous as we aspire towards the essential. It is always possible to express truths, personal convictions or powerful, fleeting pleasures in a more succinct way. Just like the haiku, the list can represent a way of turning a selection of words and sensations into a mini work of art.

Think of the words we use as a house. Use them with as much love and care as possible to keep a trace of all the little nothings which make up our lives.

Lists or diaries?

'Soon I won't have any space for my diaries, I have so many
of them in different shapes and sizes. I hide them in boxes, in
suitcases, behind the curtains, under beds, even in a cot
in the attic which had been empty for a long time... A
cleaner came to help me wrap them in old sheets... we
sewed up the sheets and I called these packages "mummies"
and wrote on them the date on which I'd made them.
To confuse nosy people, I stacked the "mummies"
in boxes and wrote "white laundry" on them.'

A twenty-four-year-old woman in *On Diary*, accounts collected by
Philippe Lejeune

In the past, keeping a diary was seen almost as a moral obligation. In some countries, like Japan, many people still practise this ritual. No one asks what the point is. It is simply something people do, something people have always done. People think that if they don't keep a diary, they will let a precious part of life slip through their fingers. In my native France, teenagers and older people still keep diaries, but the practice is becoming rarer. People see it as old-fashioned and swotty, as a tedious obligation. Broadcasting your personal life to strangers on the internet, by writing a blog, is seen as a far more worthwhile activity – as though what gives life meaning is other people's validation. There is no question that the diary is no longer the mode of expression best suited to our times.

The second disadvantage of the diary is that it is, by nature, too intimate. You're at the mercy of indiscreet glances, you live in fear of being read. (The exception here is the Japanese practice of couples' diaries, where the partners will write down things they want the other to know, so feelings are revealed without face-to-face confrontation.) A diary can become overwhelming; it can take up too much space, both physically and psychologically. Some people crumble under the weight of a lifetime's diaries, and worry more about what will happen to their diaries when they die than about what will happen to them.

So what's to be done if you feel as though your diaries are weighing you down? It would be a shame to get rid of so much of your lived experience; perhaps the solution could be to go back over your entries and edit them (delete certain things, rewrite others), to extract the best things, the words of wisdom. And then, with the help of lists, you can rewrite your life in a simpler, less wordy way. Allow your experiences to breathe. Include headings, for example, 'small panoramas of my life', 'travel notes', 'my misadventures', 'my best memories'... And let go of the rest: the burdensome emotions, the entreaties, sighs and tears... Tidy up your writing in the same way you'd tidy a house which has been left empty for so long you have no idea what it harbours. A house which contains so many excessive, sterile, useless things that you no longer have room to live and breathe.

Training yourself to rewrite the events of your personal life in a new style can help you to detach from certain things, to remove the cloak of drama or tragedy which covered them. You will lighten your mental and emotional burden and seize the essence of what life has taught you; this in turn will allow you to move forward. Of course this task may stir things deep inside you, and may entail symbolic deaths. But, in the end, life will emerge victorious. The key to living well is learning lessons, then continuing on your way. Make this experience of personal decluttering a stimulating, reinvigorating thing. Reworking your memories will also make them clearer and more accessible.

The concise form of the list will make the work of collecting facts and statements a lot easier, more practical and more pleasant. Your emotions will reattach themselves to the names, events and places as you rewrite them. They will be anchored in us far more firmly than we could previously have imagined.

Lists allow us to rethink and restructure our ideas. They give us a panoramic view of our lives. They breathe fresh life into our writing, make the important things more visible, make rereading a pleasure. Ozu's *Diaries 1936–1963* are a marvellous example of this practice. When he described a day as 'Siesta', what he meant was that he'd been on a bender the night before.

Do not leave overly intimate writing behind, but instead keep a record of the gifts life has given you. Make this your life's work: this is the compromise between keeping a diary and leaving nothing to posterity.

A creative hobby for everyone

'I polish my poems alone
In the darkening day.'

Haiku by Kyoshi Takahama

Writing the book of your life in the form of lists can be the most accessible hobby. It is the most constructive activity imaginable, as fulfilling as crosswords, if not more so. And the same can be said whether you're seven or 117.

Life is boring for people who do nothing: you get the impression of not living. Laziness and boredom make time shrink; when we are bored we do not fill our time and, in hindsight, time seems shorter. But by living fully, time can stretch almost to infinity.

Lists prove that any of our lives can be interesting or dull, that what matters is the depth of our perception. The lists of a recluse could be utterly fascinating.

You'll never get bored writing lists

Making lists is a way of entering your own private realm. It allows you to define the terms of your own life, to name its guiding concepts and ideas. As soon as you do so, you will forget your surroundings, your external circumstances and the uncertainties of everyday life.

Spending your moments of leisure writing notes on the books you've read, transcribing conversations you've had, noting down snippets of knowledge, contemplating the ethics and aesthetics of a perfect life, formulating your exact idea of happiness, searching for meaning, visualising your goals, your highest aspirations and the means by which you might achieve them… these activities are fascinating in and of themselves. They are also accessible to everyone. They allow us to rise up, to reach – and surpass – our potential. And life can so easily drag us down…

Writing lists doesn't require any concerted effort, particular talent or constraints. Simply follow the flow of your ideas. The practice will give life to your thoughts, to your own style, to your own existence. This collection of writing will, as day follows day, become our personal bible, the reflection of our inner life, a focal point that will allow us to recover the unity, the harmony, the simple sense of wonder, which we otherwise tend to lose.

Become master of a secret, limitless treasure

The passion some people have for lists can also be explained by the desire to be completist. They think the world, once written down, can be mastered. The world is more knowable, it is better suited to their needs. Everything now seems less immense, less complex, less strange — less worrying. They have a sense that they and their lives now fit better in the world.

A book of lists is priceless. It contains our lives, it is proof of our creativity and it has been written by our own hand. The older it is and the fuller it is, the more value it has. After ten years, according to the Japanese, it will be a treasure, and the joys it will bring will be incomparable.

PART ONE

LISTS TO SIMPLIFY
EVERYDAY LIFE

1

Time is money

Time-saving lists

'Every day is a treasure. Do not compare it to a
dragon's bright pearl. A dragon's pearl can be found.
But even if we lived for one hundred years, this day
could not be lived again.'

Master Dogen, Bonze Zen (1200–1253)

What are our lives if not the hours we possess? How do we use them?

Lists are a practical way of saving time when we feel overwhelmed by everything we have to do or want to do.

I am not denying that spontaneity has its charms. But very often, it is necessary to be organised in order to take full pleasure from your time and enjoy all the opportunities life presents. Writing down what we earn and what we spend allows us to make adjustments, to reduce the outgoings which do not bring value to our lives. In the same way, writing down what we have to do allows for a greater degree of organisation and enables us to make conscious choices (as with many other things in life, realising is half the battle).

In the course of a day, we scribble things down anywhere and everywhere, a thousand and one little nothings. We think we are regulating our frenetic lives. These small mementos are soothing: we no longer 'have to remember'. We tick off what we have done, and these little ticks give us a sense of satisfaction. We have achieved something.

Of course, for those of us who work, writing a list of priorities for the day or the week is a helpful way of making the most of our time. We all know that making a list of tasks at the beginning of the working day will help us make progress in the most productive way. At every minute of every day, ideas and intentions surge into our brains like flashing red lights. And this is not good for our memory. This constant rush of stimuli creates background anguish. And this, in turn, damages our quality of life. To avoid crumbling under the strain, it is important, especially at work, to sort what is important from what is not. Do not proceed to the next email in your inbox until you have replied to or deleted the previous one. Make a 'To Do' list and tick the tasks off as you go along, even if it's just ironing or doing your nails.

Don't put anything off to the next day. Apart from the stress caused by not having dealt with what you know you should have dealt with, putting something off is a form of avoidance. And avoidance leads to failure. Getting a chore done is the best way of forgetting it. And there are other benefits: the feeling of having overcome difficulty is good for your morale. If boredom is the cause of your procrastination, begin by doing the thing you least want to do. If the cause is the size of the task, then break it down.

Knowing that you have control over your time brings relief and a real feeling of comfort. We know that nothing will slip through the net. Writing a 'To Do' list is an official declaration of what we must achieve. Writing down the different steps of a task helps us. Lots of small tasks are less overwhelming, psychologically, than one large task. This is one of the benefits of making lists.

Creative people are particularly good at organising their lives, at choosing what they do, at making time work hard for them. This is because they are sensitive to the importance of rhythm in everyday life, and this rhythm is every bit as important for their health as it is for their productivity and efficiency. For them, a schedule is not a constraint. It's a way of listening to their bodies.

Making lists of your activities follows the same principle: organising your time to maximise positive experiences while living in the way which suits us best. The key principle is to find a way of life which corresponds best to our needs. This allows us to maximise our quality of life.

Suggested lists:

Things which occupy most of my time

Moments of 'me time'

The time I have to enjoy what I own, and the time I spend earning the means to acquire it

Things which waste my time (calls which go on too long, information overload)

Things I regret having done because they wasted my time

Things I regret not having done

Times when I really lived in the moment

Times when I really wasn't in the moment

Time spent on household chores, on cooking (including shopping, tidying, washing up)

Time spent at work (including your commute)

Time you have to yourself (for example, for yoga, meditation, writing)

Time spent with my nearest and dearest (including email-writing and calls).

Make the most of your time

Every 'today' well lived turns 'yesterday' into a golden memory.

To work on time is to work on yourself. You're walking – you don't know where you're walking to, exactly – but you're walking to feel alive. Or you're stretched out in a field watching the clouds pass, admiring the water in a stream. Or you're spending a Sunday afternoon lying back in your armchair or snuggled deep in bed reading a thriller. What could possibly be more important than these things? The mere fact of stopping time, of giving yourself permission to be lazy, allows you to rediscover the relativity of time, to feel the flow of it, without being controlled by it.

Sometimes rituals can help. They help you to concentrate, to focus your attention, to sweep the mental cobwebs away. They help you to banish your internal tensions and find yourself again. They mark the before and the after. They help you to move between tasks seamlessly.

TO BE MASTER OF YOUR TIME, YOU CAN:

Plan your priorities for the week.

Plan, months in advance, health check-ups and appointments with the dentist, the hairdresser and the optician (or days in advance, depending on the country you live in).

Collect all the information you need *before* you start a project.

Make your goals time-specific. *I will finish this in a week, a month, and so on.*

Always have your lists to hand. Make sure they are clear and up to date.

Do the housework on Saturday. That leaves Sunday free. Make a list of your chores before you start.

When you have a day off, have a lie-in.

Take an indulgently long bath (music, candles, bath oils).

Have a proper breakfast. Make yourself a real coffee, put bread under the grill, read the papers.

Plan your meals in advance.

Group your tasks (e.g. things to buy in a certain part of town, letters and emails to write, calls to make, visits to make).

Laugh.

Look at nature.

Drink half what you would have. Twice as often.

Bake.

Go to bed earlier. Get up earlier.

Turn up to meetings early.

When you have time, have a picnic.

Go for a walk for the sheer pleasure of it.

Do it, don't procrastinate. (Doing nothing is the most time-consuming thing in the world. Doing things takes far less time.)

Own as little as you can (that way you're not constantly buying or cleaning or looking after or getting rid of things).

Only spend time with your real friends.

Only do one sport (it doesn't matter if it's walking, jogging or yoga, it doesn't have to be a team sport).

Turn off your television.

Spend less time on your phone.

Be precise in your arrangements: set a date, a place, a time.

Clear up after yourself.

Only retain useful information.

Wear clothes which are easy to take care of and to match (twinsets, suits, top halves and bottom halves in the same colour).

Learn to say no (spend time with yourself instead).

Now, over to you…

Suggested lists:

Keyboard shortcuts

Favourite websites

Email addresses

Passwords and PIN codes

Contact details for service providers (for contracts, complaints…).

Five ways to take the
stress out of Christmas

November is the best time to start thinking about Christmas. Make lists. If you try to keep everything in your head, you'll have to start from scratch again the next Christmas. If you make lists, you'll only have to update them.

SMALL PIECES OF ADVICE

Buy your cards the first week of December. If you write them early enough, you won't have to rush them or worry about them. Instead, you will take pleasure in writing them.

Set an exact budget which includes presents, food, decorations and invitations. Make it a round number, for example £500 or £1,000. This way, you won't have to worry about your credit card bill in January. Go shopping early in the month to avoid the crowds; if possible, buy your presents throughout the year (on holiday, at craft fairs, and so on). By doing this, your gifts will be original. Also, you won't be tempted to buy things for yourself at a time of year when everyone is in a consumerist frenzy. Make a list of potential presents which aren't objects (this will also save you from too much wrapping). Try to think of useful presents, presents which match the individual needs of the people on your list. Think of 'minimalist' presents: clever, non-material presents (a massage or treatment, a wine-tasting evening, cinema membership, subscription to a magazine, a haircut, a trip in a hot air balloon…). Give gifts which will genuinely allow the recipient to broaden their horizons, or to pursue their tastes and passions.

Make putting up decorations a social event. For example, get your family together one weekend, and perhaps that will be one of your most special Christmas memories.

Keep the menu simple. Remember that, in all the excitement, everything will be eaten quickly.

Make sure you have a case of good wine to hand so that you have something to bring if you receive a last-minute invitation.

Equally, put together a box of small gifts so you always have something ready as a thank you to a neighbour or a gift for a child. (Old Japanese people always carry a little something, already wrapped, in their bag – a handkerchief, a small box of green tea, a fan, a biscuit, a keyring – to give to someone who helps them.)

Keep a box containing good-quality notepaper, postcards, birthday cards, stamps, photos you may like to send, different sizes of envelope, a coloured pen, Sellotape and odds and ends of wrapping paper.

Suggested lists:
Cards to be sent
Cards you've received
Your budget for celebrations (including dinners, outings, presents, the cost of postage)
New Year resolutions.

Presents

Is there anything simpler than writing down what you have given and what you have received? Keep a presents list – it will represent all the love and friendship in your life!

Suggested lists:

Presents received (date, an exact description)

Presents given (date, price, description)

Special occasions in the year to come

Ideas for presents to give yourself

Ideas for original, personalised gift wrapping.

Keep your accounts up to date: my *kakebo*

'A person who gets used to buying unnecessary things is often a person in need.'

Hannah Farnham Sawyer Lee, *Three Experiments of Living*

Out of all the lists we keep, the one which is most often kept, read and reread is a list of our finances. Who can say they have never kept one?

In Japan, this habit is learnt in primary school; as soon as children learn to count they are taught to keep a little book of accounts. Everyone must bring to school a small amount of money, their pocket money, and they must learn to manage it by writing down precisely what they have spent, how much they have left and what to do if not much is left. Has this contributed to the country's economic success?

A good number of Japanese women take their *kakebo* incredibly seriously. Every day they write in it not only their incomings and outgoings but also recipes they see on cooking programmes (they leave a special space for this on the double spread for the week), their marital disputes (in case of divorce proceedings, having exact facts and dates comes in useful!), visits to the doctor (it's very useful to keep a record of how diseases evolve), visits to the hairdresser, presents received and presents given, and so on. They devote two pages to each week, and at the end write a summary of the week. And, in turn, a summary of the month and of the year.

This is how they plan the family budget, save up for their children's education, for their children's weddings, for leisure pursuits and for their retirement. Their *kakebo* represents the best way of managing their material, marital, family and social life. It is also the best way of managing their time and allowing themselves true moments of leisure. This method has contributed to the economic success of the country. Some claim that the *kakebo* method has allowed them to make savings of at least ten per cent.

For these perfect housekeepers, money and time aren't commodities to be used or abused on a whim. Not making lists simply is not an option for them. For them, managing money and time is a way of life. And, in the harsher times our ancestors experienced, wasn't the same true?

Suggested lists:

Things I buy which I know I don't need

Outgoings in the next twelve months

My most memorable and extravagant purchases

My incomings and outgoings (including the money I put aside into savings)

What I want to buy

What I need

What I want to buy right now (write this down on the back of a receipt and keep it in your purse. The impulse will probably pass).

2

Cooking and food

Recipes and kitchen tricks

'A halibut from the deep, cold seas
Which, with bread,
I devoured piece by piece.'

Haiku by Kusama Tokihiko

Shopping lists, meal plans, recipes… I've written hundreds of these in my life. Keeping a list of recipes which you have already tried, perfected and enjoyed in a single book will save you the trouble of looking through heavy cookbooks. Cookbooks take up space in your home. They tend to contain more photos than text, and more recipes which don't interest us than recipes which do.

In the past, our grandmothers would keep books of recipes and these would be an invaluable inheritance, not only for the culinary instructions but also for the memories and emotions they evoked. I do not have such a book, but I do have, in my spiral-bound notebook, a section for recipes. It contains my favourite dishes, the recipes my family and friends have given me, as well as recipes I have come up with myself. When I want to experiment, I consult the internet, or I ring my mother or my friends. I organise my recipes under the headings 'substantial meals', 'light meals', 'desserts', 'Mum's recipes', 'Chiyo's recipes' (she's a Japanese friend of mine, and an excellent cook). I mark each recipe with the name of the person who passed it on, and the date. 'Catherine's gobo udon noodles, Oakwood, 2005', 'John's split pea soup, 2003, it was snowing in Bronxsville', and I think of those people, and the moments we shared when they cooked me those meals.

I also keep in this section charts of nutritional information, of weights and measures and, finally, a list of 'kitchen tricks', things I tend to forget but which are very useful on certain occasions (for example, make one-millimetre notches on potatoes before you cook them then, when they're cooked, plunge them into a bowl of cold water and ice, so you can peel them very quickly; or knead the meat in cornflour to make it more tender).

Suggested lists:

Meals for one
TV dinners
Romantic meals
Family meals
Meals with friends
Celebratory meals
Dinner parties
Tea o'clock
Sunday-night dinners

10-minute meals

Picnics

Meals to eat in the garden

Packed lunches

Low-calorie meals

Healing meals (after indigestion, liver problems etc)

Meals for rainy days.

HOW TO IMPROVISE A MEAL

You should always have the ingredients to hand to throw together one or two meals (frozen vegetables, herbs etc). This way you are prepared for unexpected guests, illness or bad weather. Keeping a list of these meals will help you not only to make sure you always have the ingredients available, but will also help you make plans for these throw-together meals: soup or a starter, cheese, bread and dessert.

My gastronomic notebooks

MY GOURMET ALMANAC

Why not write yourself a 'gourmet almanac', reflecting the changing of the seasons? Make it detailed, month by month, including the fruits and vegetables which are in season, dishes which are appropriate for the weather (spaghetti bolognaise and red wine, perhaps, on a rainy night).

I will always remember one list. A Japanese woman wrote down everything she cooked for her husband in sixty years of marriage, tailoring each meal to his age and health, to the demands of his body and the changes it was undergoing. This list became the subject of a documentary, broadcast on national television. It represented the ideal guide to cooking, both as a dietary model and a proof of love.

PAIRINGS

It's fun to write a list of your favourite food and drink pairings. This list will spare you from eating anything and everything. It will allow you to treat yourself to the things you really like. If you are sure of your tastes, you will not only have the pleasure of enjoying these pairings, but also of anticipating them and of accepting nothing less.

Writing a list of your favourite pairings – for example, Darjeeling tea with scones, mussels with beer, a glass of champagne with a boiled egg, a glass of Bordeaux with pâté – is an exercise in creativity. Why not write these pleasures in the form of haikus, adding the ideal backdrop for them (the music, the venue, the lighting, the occasion, the person sharing that particular pleasure with you)?

MY GASTRONOMIC MEMORIES

What a shame it is to lose the memory of certain meals. Generally we don't write down what we eat, even if we keep a diary, and yet special meals can form some of the best moments of our lives. Recording the place, the food, the wine and the people present is a way of rekindling these exceptional memories.

MY FAVOURITE RESTAURANTS AND THE WALKS I TAKE AFTERWARDS

Make a list of your favourite restaurants. And think of routes for pre- or post-dinner strolls. Restaurants and routes should go hand in hand. So many pleasures can be multiplied with a little imagination and time.

CAFÉS, BARS, CLUBS, TEA HOUSES, PLACES TO GO WINE-TASTING

These places often have memorable names. Once you have visited them, they become a part of you – bistros in Paris, grand hotel bars in New York, shacks on tropical beaches… For a bit more 'spice', record the name of the wheat beer or the dark chocolate you lingered over in these places, along with the people you shared that moment with (even the people you didn't know, but simply observed).

MY FAVOURITE PRODUCTS

In this list you can include the best olive oils you can find at the market, the name of the ham you tasted at a friend's house… as well as the names of specialist delicatessens, of renowned bakeries you read about in magazines. It is better to buy a few high-quality ingredients than lots of cheap produce. But in order to do so, you have to become a connoisseur. These shop names will also come in very handy when you need to buy presents. But buying the best of certain things doesn't prevent you from researching how to buy basic produce as cheaply as possible. And that is how you combine gastronomy and economy.

THE PLEASURES OF THE CELLAR

A list of the wines you have enjoyed – where, when, with whom. A Japanese friend describes each wine he tries by comparing them to people (either celebrities or people he knows).

THE MEALS I HAVE SERVED

This list will prevent repetition: you will avoid serving the same meals to the same people. You may also get ideas for new guests – the meals we have eaten as guests can provide inspiration for what we serve next. In *ryokan*, a traditional Japanese setting, it is customary to receive a small menu card at the beginning of the meal (which is always unique). What a lovely custom! Not only do these cards remind you of what you have eaten, but they also allow you to plan, according to your appetite, what to leave on your plate so you can fully savour the next course. Why not try this: leave menu cards on your guests' plates, and say on the card that they shouldn't feel obliged to eat everything. Before a Japanese tea ceremony, the master will invite his guests by letter, in beautiful penmanship. He will begin by evoking the weather and the season, then list the invitees, the time and the menu which will be served. These letters, written in ancient Japanese style, are sometimes true works of art.

Suggested lists:

Ideas for last-minute meals, and for non-perishable ingredients
to keep in your cupboards

Places which deliver

Meals appropriate for certain conditions (for example,
diabetes, cholesterol, heart problems)

Epicurean nights (write down the type of music, glassware,
drink, and lighting to accompany each dish)

The pairings which give me pleasure

My best gastronomic memories

My favourite restaurants, and the walks which go with them

Bars, bistros, tea houses, wine-tasting bars

My favourite products

The pleasures of the cellar

What I have served my guests.

3

Health, diets and beauty

The health notebook

'Your body is your vehicle for life. As long as you are here, live in it. Love, honor, respect and cherish it, treat it well and it will serve you in kind.'

Suzy Prudden

In theory, everyone collects recipes. But how many of us write down everything about their health and well-being in a 'body book'? If you track signs of weakness, record them, read them and reread them, you will train your subconscious to send a warning every time you neglect yourself or let yourself go.

This practice is also useful for diagnosing the beginnings of certain diseases, and being able to tell your doctor exactly when and how your symptoms developed. You can also keep a list of recipes to help with different health conditions, for example, colds or indigestion, ulcers or sore throats.

Suggested lists:

The illnesses I have suffered (dates, symptoms, durations)

The operations I have had

Medication I have taken in the past

Medication I am currently taking

The causes of my health problems

Things I could do to improve my health and don't

My biorhythms (when I get hungry, when I sleep, when I get tired)

The ways in which I abuse my body

The things I should have stopped eating a long time ago and
   haven't

The things I really need to stay in top condition

The meals I should make

The hours I should keep

The rules I should set myself and stick to

The treatments, cures and therapies I have undergone

My recipes for illness and for health

Foods which raise cholesterol

Foods which are bad for diabetes

Foods which are thought to be excellent for different illnesses.

Conversations with my body

'Eat less meat and more vegetables
Add less salt and more vinegar
Eat less sugar and more fruit
Take small mouthfuls and chew slowly
Wear light clothes and take frequent baths
Avoid idle talk and commit to lifelong learning
Control your desires and compliment others
Keep your mind free of worries and sleep soundly
Walk, don't take the car
Never get angry and smile all the time.'

Words printed on an old Japanese tea cup

Lists allow us to discover the psychological causes of illnesses, and even change the course of them. Making a list of conversations to have with your body will help you to understand the role we play in catching illnesses. Our bodies send us messages when they are in need of attention. Noticing and listening to these messages helps us to take action to overcome health problems. All these signals are trying to do is rouse us from our passivity, from the lack of responsibility we are taking for our bodies.

One approach would be to write a list in two columns, to begin a conversation with the ideal, healthy you. Ask why it has become trapped inside you. Try to stay in touch with it as often as possible. A list of these dialogues will help you; it will courier messages between you and your ideal self.

Keep this list on your person, creating a physical link between the list and your body, an intimate connection between the words it contains and your subconscious.

You can also make this sort of 'dialogue list' to better understand your problems with alcohol, tobacco, drugs and other forms of addiction, even your problems with tiredness. Tiredness is often a symptom of failing to spot something that is distressing or worrying us. Instead of submitting to inertia, write a dialogue between yourself and your fatigue, in the form of a list. This will help to decode your body's signals, and find the culprit (backache, apathy, lethargy, and so on).

Suggested lists:

Conversations between the healthy me and the me who is
    imprisoning it

Conversations between the me who doesn't drink (or take
    drugs or smoke), and the addict me

Conversations between the well me and the ill me

Conversations between me and my tiredness.

The dieting notebook

'One portion is enough
I wash my rice.'

Haiku by Santoka Taneda

Countless books have been written about dieting: get-thin-quick advice, psychological advice... But why not come up with a book which is tailored to your own body, a dieting book which will allow you to identify what works for you and what doesn't? You will find no better dieting coach than this document. What do you eat? When? Where? How much? And in what state of mind?

Recording your weight and writing down what you eat is just as beneficial as recording your finances. But is setting a target weight the best way of going about dieting? Most people want to lose weight and are disappointed when this doesn't happen. Writing down vague aspirations will not do the trick. You need to be precise about what you want. Writing positive thoughts will only help deliver a new reality if you are prepared for it. This sort of writing demands a lot of precision and focus. You must be rigorous when you choose the words you use to express what you want. If you write: 'I want everything in my life to get better', your life, in all probability, will not improve. The 'everything' is far too vague. Your subconscious has no idea how to interpret this. Be more precise. Write 'I want to stop eating (give an example)' or 'I want to lose ten kilograms' or 'I want to walk ten kilometres three times a week'.

Your objectives should be measurable: exactly how many

kilograms do you want to lose? And in what timescale? How will you lose them? (By changing your diet? By doing more exercise? By visualising your ideal self?) If this is written down, your goals will filter into your subconscious, especially if you frequently reread what you have written in your notebook.

Your goals should be realistic. Otherwise you are doomed to failure. Write a list of your motivations. Only set yourself goals which you can influence. Then turn words into action. One action will lead to another. The things *you* have written in *your* notebook will carry a lot more weight than the things you read in books and magazines. Writing lists is the first step towards really becoming the master of yourself. No doctor can make you lose weight: they can only advise it.

Set out your personal weight-loss programme by writing a list of the advice you have been given: by your doctor, by your friends, by the books you have read.

This list will allow you to compare techniques, to identify contradictions and to put yourself at the centre of things. You will probably already know everything a dietician may tell you. Lists are your best ally. Weighing yourself every day, and recording your weight, can make a huge difference to your eating habits. Here is a list of suggested topics, but you must write your own, bespoke lists to achieve the results you want.

Suggested lists:
My weight, day to day, on a calendar which also shows the
    phases of the moon (the electromagnetic properties of the
    moon influence everything in nature: the tides, the weather,
    tectonic plates)

How much I spend on diet food and weight loss

My favourite low-calorie meals

My recipes, by season

The diets I've tried

My dieting mistakes

My motivations to lose weight

How I would ideally like to look (go into as much detail as possible: hair, make-up, accessories, colours, clothes)

The things I would like to change about my appearance

My calorie chart

The downsides of carrying extra weight

The money I'm going to spend on losing weight

Diets and weight-loss methods which are dangerous to your health (making yourself sick, fasting without suitable preparations, throwing yourself into mono-diets etc)

The reasons why I eat when I'm not hungry

How I ate as a child

The challenges I need to expect (not becoming disheartened by plateaus in my weight loss, not forgetting that a body has to get accustomed to its new weight)

The best way of visualising my new self, to encourage weight loss

My anxieties about food

My obsessions.

Sketch your exercise

Recently, I had a happy surprise. I discovered, folded and tucked away in a book about yoga, an A3 sheet showing all the poses the book described, in sketch form.

That gave me the idea of making lists of sketches for other types of exercise. When folded in eight, the paper on which I draw these sketches is exactly the same size as my organiser. These documents are very useful indeed after a few months of letting yourself go, and now they take pride of place next to my other lists. Even if I haven't done my sun salutation or my moon salutation for… hmmm… a few weeks, at least I know where to find the poses, and seeing them folded up in my organiser reminds me of how lazy I've become.

Suggested lists:

Yoga poses

Kinaesthetic exercises (to be done on your commute, in front of your computer or while cooking)

Face massages (to be done while you're devoting time to your skin)

Head massage (to be done while you're washing your hair).

Beauty secrets

Without keeping this list, how much advice might one forget! Home-made beauty masks, mini detox fasts at the beginning of each season – you can make yourself a compendium of all the things you find effective, pleasant and trustworthy (advice from your nearest and dearest, from your yoga instructor, from your dance teacher…). These lists can form the perfect complement to a diet. It's good to slim down, but to slim down while becoming more beautiful is even better…

Suggested lists:

Skincare

Haircare

How to take care of your nails

How to take care of your body

The benefits of water

Food and drink to improve your appearance.

4

Housework

Domestic routines

Seiri (get rid)
Seiton (tidy)
Seiso (clean)
Seiketsu (order)
Sktisuke (rigour)

Developing a domestic routine helps you keep your house in order. Do a few small chores every day instead of trying to do everything in one go. If you have a daily list of tasks to complete, you won't end up feeling lost, having no idea where to start, what to do when and where, and the feeling of disorder won't get to you. Because it will get to you! Coming up with a precise method will prevent you from getting distracted, from feeling that you haven't done enough or have forgotten something. Following a routine and sticking to it, knowing the end result will be good, will turn chores into a sort of game. Or a ritual which can bring you satisfaction without the need for soul-searching.

Why not come up with a daily routine in which you do five things, each lasting fifteen minutes? So, for fifteen minutes: hoover, dust, clean the bathroom, and so on. (Be warned: the rooms which require the most attention are not the biggest rooms, but the ones which are used most often, for example, the kitchen or the bathroom.)

Make a list of what needs to be done in each room. This will help you psychologically. You'll have so much more energy in a tidy, well-kept room. Time spent on housework is never wasted, whatever some people may think. You can also write a 'How To' list along the lines of a recipe. There are solutions to every housework problem, solutions which don't require much time or money. As long as you know the secrets. And remember them...

FOR EXAMPLE, HOW TO:

Make your fridge smell good
Clean a sofa
Get rid of ants
Use environmentally friendly cleaning products.

15 STEPS WHICH TAKE 15 MINUTES

1. Tidy the room (get rid of things lying around; you should always begin by tidying).
2. Open the curtains and windows to air the room.
3. Charge your phone.
4. Put the dirty laundry in the basket.
5. Put the washing on.

6. Empty the bins.
7. Do the dishes.
8. Clean the bathroom and the loo.
9. Make the beds.
10. Fluff up the cushions.
11. Sweep and/or hoover.
12. Water the plants and change the water in vases.
13. Wipe the table and other surfaces you often use.
14. Look in the fridge and see what's for dinner.
15. Write a shopping list and a 'To Do' list.

A WEEKLY DOMESTIC ROUTINE

Change your sheets (and sort your linen).

Hoover the rugs.

Wipe down the kitchen and the bathroom.

Disinfect the toilet (keep gloves which you use only for this task).

Check you have enough clean clothes and underwear for the week ahead.

If necessary, place an online order for heavy groceries.

Throw away out-of-date food from your fridge and cupboards.

Stock up the fridge for the coming week (and no longer).

Do the ironing.

MONTHLY CHORES

Wipe, dust and make the floor shine.

Wash the windows.

Wax wooden surfaces. This will protect the wood and make
them smell nice.

Dust or hoover under the beds, the sofa, other furniture.

Get rid of empty toiletries from your bathroom.

Throw out the newspapers, magazines and post which you
have already read.

Clean the oven.

Have a little waltz with a duster in your hand. Check there are
no spiders' webs.

Turn over your mattresses.

Do all the laundry.

Clean the hinges on doors and windows. Dust builds up there.
And the skirting boards.

The annual spring clean

Take your duvets, blankets and curtains to be steam-cleaned. Sort through everything you own or, if you can afford to, enlist a professional service for a day and… go for a walk.

Suggested lists:
'How To' lists
My daily housework routines
My weekly housework routines
My monthly housework routines
My lists of tasks to delegate to X.

Fixed lists and provisional lists

You can write lists about practically anything: lists of errands, lists of parties to look forward to, lists of things to plant in your garden. But if some lists need to be rewritten every time you use them, others can be used several times. We can improve and refine them. For example, your list of things to take on holiday. You could take this list away with you and improve it as you go along, for example, by making a note of what you have used and what you haven't. Keep this list in your suitcase. It will help you the next time you go away.

Suggested lists for keeping:

Things to take on holiday

Things to take on weekends away

Things to take to the pool, to the sports club

Things to take on picnics, on camping trips

The objects and furnishings in your house (if possible with photos of how they were when you bought them, and receipts – this can be very useful if you have any problems with them)

Lists of chores for every member of the family.

5

Getaways

Plan ahead for better travel

'Above the coconut trees
The dawn of spring
Where my heart journeys.'

Haiku by Oguma Kazunda

When we are tired, we are no longer capable of calling upon our usual ways of organising our lives, and this is when we are most in need of going away and relaxing. Having a small list of 'getaways' ready (including, for example, phone numbers for hotels or country inns, the logistics of getting there, the places to visit and the activities on offer, the prices…) can be an invaluable safety net. Even the telephone number of a little boutique hotel could offer a refreshing alternative when you need a change of scene. Gather information on potential getaways and make plans to put your ideas into action. If you want to go to Rome, start a file called 'Rome'. Gather all the necessary information for a last-minute getaway. You can also plan a little surprise trip for your partner, or for a parent or friend. If you tell them everything is already planned, they are more likely to agree. 'Getaway' lists are the best sort of list for your morale; by opening future avenues, they help you cope with day-to-day reality.

Suggested lists:

Weekend or holiday getaways

Friends who have invited you to visit

The research to do to get to such-and-such a place.

Travel preparations

No matter what sort of trip you're going on, whether big or small, make a list of everything you need to do and take before you set off. A good, trusty list will give you peace of mind and a sense of calm. And this in turn will free up the mental space to enjoy the pleasures of getting away.

You can make lists for any type of break: winter breaks, summer breaks, holidays in the mountains, at the beach, holidays in warm countries, in cold countries, business trips... And keep lists as you go along ('I should have taken that, shouldn't have taken that...') Lists are never perfect first time around.

A LIST FOR A LONG TRIP

1. **At home:**

   Turn off the water, the gas, the electricity.

   Empty the fridge and switch it off.

   Put the rubbish out.

   Check the contents of the freezer (and empty it if you are going away for a long time. If the power goes off, say, in a storm, the results could be catastrophic).

   Check your security alarm is working before you activate it.

2. **Admin:**

   Make a photocopy of your passport, your credit cards and, if possible, your itinerary. Give them to someone close to you.

Make sure that the most important things (plane tickets, hotel reservations, credit cards – you can't rely on just having one – and enough cash) are in a bag which you will never let out of your sight.

3. Planning ahead:

Make a list of the presents you need to bring back (that will stop you buying too many or buying any old thing). Read up about the things the country you are visiting is famous for. Know what you want to bring back (it's better to buy yourself one lovely thing than a bag full of things which will lose their charm the minute you leave the shop).

Leave enough room for these presents in your suitcase or bag.

Make a list of people to send postcards to with the addresses (this will give you peace of mind while you're away).

Get your hair done, get your nails done, go to the dentist...

4. People to contact and useful services:

Make a list of the people you have to phone before you set off (business, meetings...).

Phone people to warn them you will be away (your parents, the neighbours etc).

Make arrangements for your pets to be looked after and your plants to be watered.

Arrange for the mail to be picked up.

Get someone to keep an eye on your flat.

Give a set of keys to someone you trust.

5. **Things to sort out before you leave:**

Pick up your dry cleaning and the shoes you're having
reheeled.

Check the petrol and the oil in your car.

Charge your camera.

Pay any outstanding bills.

Take out cash.

HOW TO PACK

What to bring? First, read up about the weather at your destination.
Think about what you will be doing and who you will be meeting. Make
a list of what you are going to put in your suitcase. That will give you
a better idea of what is superfluous and what is missing. Pack your
suitcase a week before you go, that way you can keep looking at what
you plan to take and perhaps reconsider certain choices. Looking at
your suitcase will also give you the pleasure of looking forward to
your trip, and half the pleasure of going away is the anticipation.

SOME ADVICE

Never underpack.

Leave room in your suitcase for your shopping.

Always bring a cardigan for the airport and the plane (whether
you're in Singapore or Moscow, the temperature of airports
is always the same).

Toiletries and medicines are essential. You don't want to waste
time on shopping once you arrive; the shampoo in hotels

generally isn't your preferred brand. Read up on what you are allowed to take with you on the aeroplane.

Suggested lists:
What to pack for
A weekend in the country
A business trip
A trip to the seaside
A trip to the mountains
A month in a hot country.

HAND BAGGAGE

Always keep the same things in the same pockets of your luggage. Decide once and for all where you are going to keep your money, your passport, your receipts, and so on. This system will allow you to change bags quickly (think of it almost like Russian dolls) and make sure that, whether you're going to the hotel restaurant or the pool, you don't have to take your bag everywhere. Designate pockets for:

Make-up
Medication
Money
Receipts
Your camera
Your passport and tickets
Brochures and business cards.

YOUR SUITCASE

Follow the same principle. Organise things by category, so that you can pack without even thinking. Every category should have its own place.

Start from the bottom of your suitcase. First jeans and jumpers, then big things like dresses and jackets. Fold up your shirts the way they were folded when you bought them. Roll up your cardigans. Put each pair of shoes in its own bag (two pairs of shoes, over and above the pair you're wearing, will be enough). Put all your small things in individual bags, and these individual bags into a bigger one, in case you're stopped at customs. Put a label on your bag, so you can know for sure that it's yours when you go to the luggage carousel.

Think about layering. And focus on dresses (they're the most practical, compact thing to bring, and you don't have to worry about matching). Take a special outfit – you never know what may happen. And a big pashmina, plus a Macintosh with detachable lining – nights in northern Italy can be rather cold...

If you have a routine for packing, you won't forget things or make mistakes. If you respect and follow your routine, satisfaction will be guaranteed.

My kitlist

SELF-CARE

My nail kit (scissors, clippers, nail varnish, nail varnish
  remover)
Shaving kit
Cotton buds
A little tin of shoe polish (on holiday, we walk more than usual).

FOR HEALTH

Disinfectant (or lavender essence)
Plasters
Antiseptic cream
Cream for bites
Painkillers
Dressings, bandages, safety pins, scissors, tweezers
Eye cream.

TOILETRIES

Toothpaste and toothbrush
A comb
Perfume
Shampoo and conditioner
A shower cap (if you use one)

Talcum powder or deodorant

A pumice stone

A hairbrush

A hairdryer

Rollers, hairspray, clips, pins, slides, turbans etc.

MAKE-UP

Mascara

Eyeliner

Eyeshadow

Blusher

Powder or foundation

Lipstick.

ELECTRONICS

An international adapter

A charger for your camera

A phone charger

An iPod or MP3 charger (if not your phone)

A laptop charger

Memory sticks.

IMPORTANT DOCUMENTS AND MONEY

Passport (or identity card)

Tickets

Insurance documents

Credit cards

Coins and travellers' cheques

Your driving licence (an international one if necessary).

SEPARATE POCKETS FOR

Every 'kit' listed above

Underwear

Shoes

Worn clothes

A 'multi-functioning' pocket (e.g. for receipts, postcards,
    brochures, reservations, notes)

Your laptop

Chargers

A big zip bag to contain all of the above.

DIFFERENT BAGS

A day bag

A dressier bag for the evenings

A carry-on for two or three days away (or to use as hand
    luggage on the plane)

A suitcase

A sports bag for going to the pool or the spa.

YOUR HANDBAG

Your phone

Your purse (always carry small change in case you need to tip someone)

A pen and a pencil (they must have lids so they don't mark your handbag; if they don't, carry a pencil case)

Lipstick

Lip gloss (which can be applied without a mirror)

A small bottle of perfume

Your keys (always have copies somewhere)

Safety pins (they often come in hotel sewing kits)

A compact

A road or city map (optional)

Your diary

Business cards

Plasters

Aspirin

Mints

A folding umbrella

A carrier bag (in case of impromptu shopping).

6

Cutting down

Own less to have enough

'A minimum put to good use is good enough for anything.'

Jules Verne, *Around the World in Eighty Days*

If you allowed yourself a moment to list everything you own, whether in your kitchen, your bathroom, your cellar or your handbag, and then wrote down the number of items by category (twenty-four teaspoons, three ladles, five bottles of shampoo, three bottles of ketchup…), you would immediately realise which things you use effectively and which you have in excess. But exercise caution: a list like that could run to 150 pages! Still, such lists are the most effective way to get rid of clutter once and for all – unless they make you an incorrigible collector! Making a list of 'my kit' will help you to own only what you really need. No more and no less. Then you will know that everything you possess, above and beyond your 'kit', is only there to give you pleasure. And then it is over to you to work out which things give you the most pleasure!

LISTS TO DECLUTTER: 'MY ESSENTIAL KIT'

Cleaning products: bleach, dishwasher powder (which also happens to clean walls and windows), cloths, hoover, brush

Kitchen utensils: pots, colander, salad bowl, mixer, chopping boards, knife, ladle etc

Linen: sheets, towels, pyjamas

Tea time: a set including a tray, a sugar bowl, a tea pot, a box for your tea, cups and saucers

For guests: spare sheets, towels, toothbrush, pyjamas (keep all this in a pillow case)

Correspondence: writing paper, envelopes, photos to send people, postcards, stamps

Self-care: (see above)

Shoe care: a brush, wax, cloths, sealant

Atmosphere: candles, vases, perfume

Bags: one bag which you put all your bags in: shopping bags, overnight bags, evening bags, bags to take on walks or to the pool, shoe bags, laundry bags for when you go away, wash bags, laptop bags, a bag for your hairdryer and so on…

Personal papers: cheque books, passport, insurance policies

Tech: cables, instructions, guarantees.

It doesn't matter what you keep the above things in, whether it's a cupboard, a box or a bag. All that matters is that you group things by category.

Suggested lists:

My most precious possessions

Things I own too many of

Things I keep which have no sentimental value

Things I could get rid of, give away or sell (divorcing yourself
from an item isn't the hardest part; making the decision is
the hardest part)

The clothes in my cupboard that I never wear

And, by contrast, my ideal wardrobe.

Say goodbye to objects from the past

'Objects are made to save the present. They are projects of sorts. Memories are made to save childhood and youth. They are a duty the adult owes the child they were. Our memory must do justice to everything our youth was. Because our youth was our apprenticeship.'

Simone de Beauvoir, interviewed in a documentary about herself and Jean-Paul Sartre, directed by Madeleine Gobeil-Noël

We may well want to declutter our lives, but what do we do with the objects which remind us of the past? Perhaps you could write a small poem to say goodbye, summing up what the object means or evokes for you. Perhaps you could take a photo before you say goodbye. If you can't throw away a jumper belonging to an ex you split from five years ago, you could write something like this:

T's blue jumper
T wore it the day we met, on the jetty
It was the colour of his eyes
I often wrapped myself in it, it smelled of him
It was comforting to have it in the house after T left
For a long time it kept my body and my soul warm.

Suggested lists:
What the objects I want to divorce remind me of
What no longer matches my taste (everyone changes!)

Things which remind me of an argument or of someone I want
    to forget
Items given to me by someone dear to me, but which clutter my
    life nonetheless
Items bought for a home which is no longer the one I live in
Gifts I want to get rid of.

Photos, cuttings and scrapbooks

PHOTOS

Photos are also a kind of list – a visual list.

Let's take a moment to remember that making lists is a way of bringing order to chaos, of categorising things.

Making prints, deleting duplicate photos, only keeping the photos which evoke truly special memories, then sorting them by the year in which they were taken, by subject or by the people captured, then gluing them to sheets of A4 paper and sliding them into plastic folders… Such an undertaking could take weeks. But imagine your joy, at the end, of watching the film of your life play before your very eyes…

If you're lazy (and financially blessed), there are even companies which will turn your photos into books of memories. But you can also make your own album by selecting only the things which are unique to you: the people, the pets, the objects… Don't be afraid of taking a pair of scissors to your photos, and only keeping the parts which interest you. Otherwise you may end up with fifty binders of photos… Curate your photos instead.

You can then stick the pictures in a scrapbook and write in a thin-nibbed pen, directly onto the photo, the place, the date and the people present. That's all that counts to keep the memory alive. But do wait until a rainy day to do this rather arduous task – or perhaps a cold winter night.

You can also sort your photos by theme. For example, you could have an album entitled 'Lovers', which you can look at in low moments and remember the pleasure life has given you.

SCRAPBOOKS

A book on lists could hardly avoid the subject of scrapbooks. Making yourself a scrapbook is a rather attractive idea, I admit. But while lists are more concise than diaries, scrapbooks are a way of recycling clutter in another form. The point of making lists is to strip away words and superfluous things, to keep only the essential.

But if you'd still like to make a scrapbook, here are some ideas: folders in which you stick documents (cinema tickets, drawings, postcards, invitations…), all sorts of everyday things with the date, the people involved, your impressions, your poems, your quotes…

Lists preceded by the number 1

Why own more than you need to, why keep things you don't use, things which burden you, physically and psychologically, which prevent items of genuine value from being used and appreciated as they ought to be? You can streamline your life by making lists of things you only need one of.

1 oil: for hair, skin, massages, nails and make-up removal

1 soap (for your body and your face)

1 vanity case containing everything you need (not much)

1 perfume (this will give you a sense of constancy, presence and loyalty)

1 ring (why weigh yourself down with more?)

1 pair of earrings (which match your ring)

1 colour of nail varnish (so your fingernails and toenails match)

1 flower in a vase (this is the essence of Zen)

1 organiser in your bag, which contains everything you could possibly need

1 diary for your handbag (which contains anything you may need, moment to moment)

1 book of lists!

1 big scarf, for the winter cold and the summer air-con

1 set of winter things: coat, boots, hat and gloves

1 outfit for spring and autumn weekends

1 statement colour per room in your house

1 type of metal for your jewellery.

ZEN ACTIVITIES

1 particular painting to dwell on in a museum

1 solo holiday

1 beauty treatment per day (this will eliminate stress)

1 cycle of films by the same director at a time (Tati,
Wim Wenders…).

OBLIGATIONS

1 day a week with no social engagements (your personal
Sabbath)

1 bank (to keep admin and papers to a minimum)

1 word (be at one in your thoughts, your words and your
actions)

1 round figure when considering making savings (£100, £1000,
£10,000)

1 ideal weight for your whole life.

FOOD AND COOKING

1 bowl (of a size which will not allow you to overeat)

1 plate or 1 meal tray

1 portion of each dish (one slice of bread, one egg, one apple)

1 soup which offers a balanced meal (with carbohydrates,
proteins and vegetables)

1 kitchen knife and 1 chopping board

1 set of crockery per person (bowl, cup, plate, placemat)

1 style of crockery (as plain as possible, so it suits a variety of different cuisines)

1 type of tea open at once (you will be able to smell it perfectly).

To help get rid of clutter, read *Les choses* by Georges Perec. Perec writes dozens of lists of 'things'. These lists will really make you realise how enslaved you are to material goods, and the relation (or lack thereof) between these goods and happiness.

THINGS WHICH COMPLICATE LIFE

Too many people in your address book

Too many useless things

Too much choice

Too much scruffiness

Too many broken promises

Too much indecision

Getting too attached.

7

A well-ordered life

Lessons from *Getting Things Done**

How do we end up with these interminable 'To Do' lists, with the feeling we will never reach the end?

Efficiency comes from peace of mind, and peace of mind can be achieved, quite simply, by having a reliable organisational system.

An open loop is an incomplete idea which goes through your head, a vague interference whether in your actions or in time itself. Taking stock of these open loops is simple. For example, ask yourself: what, at this very moment, is preventing you from concentrating entirely on this book; what is nagging at you? What are you afraid of forgetting? We make mountains out of molehills when we contemplate what we need to do, but as soon as we write these things down, they seem far more manageable.

Getting Things Done proposes the following method:

1. Round everything up
2. Deal with it

---

* *Getting Things Done: The Art of Stress-free Productivity* by David Allen (Piatkus, 2015)

3. Organise

4. Revise

5. Act.

Essentially, it comes down to frequently closing the open loops in your head, dealing with them rapidly, organising the tasks you need to achieve according to the context, keeping updating this, and most of all, DOING SOMETHING. The key is concrete action.

If your tyres need changing, the action required isn't the changing of the tyres, it's making an appointment with the garage. Or finding a garage. The more precise you make the entry on the list, the more doable the task will seem.

If you can do something in two minutes, do it immediately. That way, it won't take up space on your list. With this rule in place, you will have the feeling that you're going at 200 km per hour, because you'll be able to solve all sorts of little problems in a single day, as well as longer and more complex tasks.

Your organiser is sacred. Only write actions in it which come with precise dates and times. Then class your entries under headings like 'Shopping in X district', 'Things to do this week', 'Phone calls to make', 'Letters to write', and so on.

Match activities, for example, 'Write a letter to Lily in the dentist's waiting room', or 'Call H while I'm at the garage getting the tyres changed'.

Finally, make a list of tasks which are easy to do, useful but non-essential, like tidying your desk or sorting through bills. Dedicate a little time to 'sweeping up' the items which stubbornly refuse to be ticked off. This is an excellent way of lifting your spirits and giving yourself the energy to finish everything on your list.

Write down your problems

Making lists is not just about writing down what you need to do. It's also about transcribing the thoughts that go through your head, so you can see more clearly what needs to be done immediately and what can wait. That way you are in a better position to identify and achieve your priorities.

Once you have transferred everything you want to get out of your head onto a piece of paper, you will feel a remarkable sense of relief. If you have problems you need to mull over or resolve, whether professional problems, relationship problems, private problems or health problems, write them down. In doing so, they will seem less important, less emotionally weighted. They will be specific, concrete and finite, easier to control, less invasive. They will just be like everything else – simply things to be fixed.

So write down all your problems, each and every one, even though you currently have no intention of trying to solve them. This list will take a huge weight off your shoulders.

Suggested lists:
Things that are worrying me
Things I fear
My problems.

Lists of questions

Before buying or renting a house or apartment, prepare a list of questions, and ask other people to help you compile it. The more questions you have prepared, the less chance there will be of nasty surprises, especially if you have to decide on the property quickly. Always try to get as much information as possible in writing.

THINGS TO ASK BEFORE RENTING OR BUYING A HOUSE OR APARTMENT

The aspect of the property

Which rooms get the sun at which times?

Daytime and night-time noise

The average cost of each utility bill

Soundproofing

Ask to turn on the taps in the sink and in the shower to check they work

Ask questions about the heating (when was the boiler installed?)

In towns, the distance to the closest public transport

The council tax band

The length of the lease or leasehold

How secure is the building?

Any problems in the neighbourhood (but make your own investigations after the visit).

You can roll this principle out into other areas which require large investments:

An operation
Buying a car
Financial investments
The working conditions at a potential employer
A bank loan
Insurance policies
Membership of a club or association.

PART TWO

LISTS FOR
SELF-KNOWLEDGE

1

Who am I?

Why try to get to know yourself better?

'Only he who knows himself is the master of himself.'

Ronsard

Writing a 'self-portrait' is a vast undertaking. You could, like Édouard Levé in his famous work *Self-Portrait*, write anything and everything that relates to you, your thoughts, your memories, your impressions. Or you could write lists of your memories. But still that would not be enough. A self-portrait must include everything about you: your past, your dreams, your tastes, your traits. Your lists, when viewed together, would paint the truest portrait of you. Lists of your recipes, the books you have read, your nightmares, your loves... the things that make you who you are.

When we observe other people, we sometimes ask ourselves whether they really know themselves, if they are really aware of what they say and what they do. But do we know ourselves any better?

Every one of us would like to possess more self-knowledge. But what we do not realise is that, when we look at ourselves, we only see what we want to see. We distort the reflection which confronts us in the mirror. We adapt it according to what society expects of us, according to our desires and our friends. By living day to day, we forget who we are in the whirlwind of life. And so we feel empty inside, constantly unsatisfied, unable to comprehend our own identity, or to find meaning in our time on the earth.

Lists allow us to choose, to remember ourselves, to reveal the depths of our true selves, to observe and reorder the disordered parts of ourselves. In this way we get to know ourselves better. We can forge an identity, and this identity is the key to knowing what we want from life.

The first virtue of writing, and especially of writing the sort of 'self-portrait' lists I advise, is to rediscover yourself, to trace with words the path which will lead you to your individual truth. We have forgotten who we are to such an extent that this path, which leads back to ourselves, seems to lead into unknown territory.

We will never know who we are because we are simultaneously one and many. But if you are modest enough to attempt this puzzle – the puzzle of the self-portrait – and to understand the importance of it, then you are at the start of a quest. This quest will be long and difficult, infinite even, perhaps impossible. But in the end it will be worth it. It is only by reflecting on the life we lead, and recognising the currents of change, that we will not miss the essential things. And that is to become aware of what life is, and of who we are.

Lao Tseu said, 'Love the world as Yourself, and then you can really love everything and Buddha. Be the light for yourself and not for the world.' This means: truly know who you are, and live as that person; develop a greater interest in your own life. That is how you fill your life with light.

Get outside yourself, observe yourself

'According to the teachings of the Talmud, we do not see things as they are but as we are. We all wear tinted glasses. One of the most important moments of our lives is when we realise we are wearing them. After we realise that, freedom seems a lot closer to us. It is a moment of great power.'

Rachel Naomi Remen, *Kitchen Table Wisdom*

In Japan, my yoga teacher would often ask us to close our eyes, to slow our minds and to gently set ourselves down next to ourselves. To observe this person who was sitting meditating. 'Observe everything about that person: their nails, their posture, their thoughts, the life they lead…' she would say, in a soft, neutral voice.

Watching is an activity in itself. It implies an observer and an observed. All it means is that the invisible 'I' is talking to the physical 'I'. By doing this exercise – and it is useful in many situations – we realise that the physical self is not in fact the focal point of our being, it is the interior self. What that self is doing, saying, thinking, feeling. By actively cultivating the ability to observe yourself, you will learn to deepen the perception of your deepest self. We need to learn how to become that observer.

What does this person look like? What choices does this person make? What are this person's passions, their loves, their past? Does this person listen to jazz? Do they have a dog? What do they tend to read? If their life were a novel, which author would have written it?

We have infinite opportunities to change our lives and actions, to find a path through the fog of our thoughts, to become aware of our place in the universe and to become more at ease with ourselves. But in order to do that, we need to draw on our past experiences and our observations of life; on what we have read and what we have thought. We must begin with as much lucidity and honesty as possible. Only then can we take a step back and realise who we truly are.

Making lists forces us to think, to interrogate, to explore, to build and to organise everything we have in terms of our personal history, our savoir-faire and our knowledge – everything we have built up in the course of our existence. All the details which we can write down will reflect an image of ourselves that is truer than the image we see in the mirror; these details will give us a new perspective on life. Then something rather magical will happen: we will begin to live in a different way; a richer, more intense, truer way. Lists have huge revelatory power. For example, if most of your friends are artists, aren't you, deep down, an artist? So why not engage in an artistic pursuit? Who knows, perhaps it will turn out to be your vocation…

The seven-faced Buddha

'Do I contradict myself? Very well then..., I contain multitudes.'

Walt Whitman, *Song of Myself*

In Japan there are 101 different types of Buddhas, among them the seven-faced Buddha. This Buddha's head is surrounded by seven faces representing the seven emotions. When we present a smiling face to the world, does it not sometimes hide anger, anxiety, sadness or bitterness? Of course we change as people, we evolve constantly, but the true self, the essence of ourselves, remains constant. So how do we discover this true self? In order to get to know yourself better, and to preserve the 'traces' of yourself – which is better than keeping objects or photos – make your own 'almanac'. The best way to do this is by keeping lists. We are one and we are multitudes. We are our true self, and we are the different selves we become in the presence of others, according to who they are and where we are... There's the self of our youth, the brave self, the fearful self, the adult self, the child self, the generous, giving self, the deceitful self, the artistic self, the honest self, the sad self, the playful self. Are we the same at a dinner party as we are at home? Are we the same person in the company of a man as we are in the company of a woman? Are we the same when we're hungry and when we're full? All these 'I's, all these 'selves', are just the different facets of our being. By creating a 'patchwork' of our multiple selves, not only in the past and present, but also in the future (the person we want or might want to become), we can catch a better glimpse of who we really are. This portrait should be as exhaustive as possible: all our selves, collected in one place (our notebook), will combine to form a portrait, a unity, a complete account, a tableau which has the power to allow us to explore our potential.

2

A monograph of me

My selves, a unique being

'We are not an average but an addition. We are not grey, we are black and white, juxtaposed, a mosaic, a duplicity.'

Saint Paul

Sometimes we have competing desires: to be married and to be single, to live in London and to live in Hawaii, to work and to retire… These internal conflicts and contradictions slow the progress of our lives. To overcome them, while remaining true to ourselves, we must strive for internal compromise and reconciliation. Writing a list of all our selves helps us to be more aware of each of them, to give each self the attention and time it deserves.

Try to capture as broad a range of the facets of your personality as you can. And then try to fold these into an integrated self, in order to best avoid external and internal conflicts. This exercise will help you to develop a greater self, which will be capable of containing all these contradictions, all these smaller, competing selves. This greater self will find novel ways of allowing them to coexist happily.

Develop the structure of this self, tease it out. Ask yourself as many questions as you possibly can; write down as many details as you possibly can. Ask yourself if you prefer company or solitude, the life you lead or the life you dreamt of twenty years ago. Write down what you like about your partner, your lover, your children and your parents. Write down what you like least about these people. Write down the clothes you like to wear, the music which speaks to you the most, the ballets which send a shiver down your spine, your moral code, your dreams...

What is love? What is success? What is happiness? What unique gift do you have to offer others? By committing a description of yourself to paper, and being able to refer to it, you will feel more 'yourself'. You will become surer in your choices and decisions; your actions will be more considered. We can find more meaning in life if we act according to our own values, so it is important to define our values. Composing your 'self-portrait' may seem a daunting task, an undertaking on an almost impossible scale. It reveals our way of life, our tastes, our morals, the workings of our subconscious and unconscious, our rational selves and our irrational selves. It reveals things we are unaware of. Who were we in our previous lives? Do we have guardian angels? Which parts of ourselves have we inherited from our ancestors and which parts reveal who we truly are?

By discovering parts of our personalities which we weren't previously aware of, we realise just how complex and multifaceted we are. And, by using lists to look at ourselves, they can tell us who we are.

Suggested lists for the different selves:

My family background

What I liked to do as a child

My qualities

My flaws

My weaknesses

My temperament

How other people see me

The person or people I want to be

My ambitions

My expectations, my regrets

The people who have influenced me

My education

My cultural heritage

My professional CV

The subjects I studied

My hobbies

My travels

The places I've lived

The places I would like to live

The types of lives I dream of leading.

My tastes

This may come as a surprise, but a good number of people do not know their own tastes. If you ask them their favourite colour or their favourite style of interior design, they'll give you a random answer, something that doesn't reflect them. A person may say their favourite colour is white, but wear brightly coloured, patterned clothes every day. They may say they prefer a modern style of interior design and live surrounded by their grandparents' furniture. But according to image consultants, knowing your favourite colour, and living in it, will make you more successful. You'll feel more yourself, more engaged, more resolute. Living this way will give you a better sense of mental harmony. You will not waste your energy on doubt, indecision and regret. You will gain internal strength by being in tune with yourself.

More proof that people don't know their own tastes is the clutter they live in. They buy things without first knowing what they love. They buy a fourth teapot, finding it prettier and more practical than the teapots they have at home, but in time they will tire of this teapot and they still won't know which of their teapots is the best. So they won't be able to get rid of any of them.

It is easier to choose between two flavours of ice cream than between twenty. In other words, life is a lot better when you know where you're going, when you know what you like and what you don't like. When you know what you want.

Suggested lists:

Places where I enjoy spending time

The types of flowers and plants I'd like to have at home

The colours I like to wear

The clothes and accessories which truly express who I am on
the inside, and which reflect my style

Clothes which are not 'me'

The make-up that suits me best

The hairstyle(s) which suit(s) me best

The activities which make me feel most fulfilled

The types of food I would like to introduce into my daily diet

My favourite style(s) of kitchenware and furniture

The sort of people I no longer want to see

The conversations I like having and hate having.

Things I would like never to do or do again

'8 March 1901, a list of things which irritate me:
People who call the silhouette of a person their 'shape'
Rolls of fat on hips
People with fish eyes
Serrated knives
Sugary wines which taste of nothing
Men with moustaches
Bananas which aren't ripe
Mad people who tell me what I want to do
Mattresses with dips in the middle.

Mary MacLane, *Diaries*

In order to know yourself, you also need to know what you don't like. Some people have grown in self-awareness by writing lists of the things which irritate them. Take, for example, Mary MacLane. A young writer from Montana at the beginning of the twentieth century, she spent seven years compiling lists not only of things she liked, but also of things she disliked.

Life demands many decisions from us, and if you don't take decisions you will never achieve anything – you will spend your life wavering. Therefore, it is good to have reasons for hating certain things and for loving others.

For your next birthday, why not write yourself a list of all the things you would rather never do again. Self-awareness comes with age, but so too does the knowledge that we won't live for ever.

In terms of your happiness, *not* doing the things you dislike is almost as important as doing the things you love. By eliminating just a few of these things, your happiness will grow. We all know the things we don't particularly like doing, but by putting them into words (especially if you're referring to types of behaviour), you become less susceptible to falling into a certain mental trap. We often do things simply because we have always done them. Our lives are, to a great extent, made up of routines. But lists help us to see our lives more clearly. It's really very simple.

Many of us have been, at different moments in our lives, uncertain about what we want for ourselves. Knowing what you don't want in your life helps you to move forward.

By listing the things you don't want to do again, you will learn where you are in your life, and knowing this is the first step towards self-awareness and self-love. You could write this list in two columns: on the left, things you have done and regretted and, on the right, what you would do differently if the same situation presented itself. The fact that the past cannot be undone doesn't make this a futile exercise. On the contrary, it is an excellent way of learning life's lessons, and reinforcing new models of behaviour which you would like to adopt.

Things I do not want in my life:

When I've wasted my time on things which have no importance
    to me (and what I'd do differently now)
Times when I've thrown happiness away
Things I don't like

Things I don't like doing

Things I can change easily

Things I can change, but with effort

Things I don't have the power to change

Types of people I wish to avoid

What I don't like about X person

What I don't like about Y context.

Japanese steps

'Life can only be understood backwards;
but it must be lived forwards.'

Søren Kierkegaard, *Papers and Journals*

Imagine a hidden garden, and in this garden there is a path of luminous stones. These stones are called 'Japanese steps', and they are there to prevent your feet from getting dirty. Imagine that these Japanese steps represent different stages in your life.

Write a list of chapter titles. For example, 'My twenties', 'My thirties', 'My forties', and so on and record under each the key events of that decade.

Ira Progoff, in *Intensive Journal*, recommends making a list of the main events of your life in this form, but he insists on the importance of creating no more than a dozen steps. This way, you will retain a clear overview of your life. These twelve steps could go something like this:

- My childhood
- My motorbike accident
- My first true love
- My marriage
- My divorce…

By chronicling your life in this way, you will be able to identify connections and correlations between events which had previously seemed disparate and unrelated (say, between your professional life and your personal life). These 'Japanese steps' will open your eyes to the person you are. It will be as though you have written your life story. You will perceive a person in flux, and that will give you an insight into how you are evolving. You can also apply the Japanese steps method to someone close to you (your partner, a friend, a member of your family...) In this way you will come to perceive them as an autonomous being, instead of seeing them as the object of your love or the fulfillment of your needs. Perhaps you will even be able to predict the next step in their story.

Lists of 'Japanese steps' can be used in different ways and applied to different spheres of your life. For example, you can do one set for your professional life and one for your personal life.

Then it will be easy to develop each of these, and add new elements. And perhaps, by reviewing the progression of your life so far, you will be able to imagine the future steps you would like to take. For example:

- My divorce has gone through
- I'm living in Nice
- I'm taking painting lessons
- I'm moving into a small, cute apartment
- I'm selling some of my paintings
- I feel as though I've finally found inner peace.

This list is also a list of wishes, but there is nothing to stop us from making these wishes come true. What you write down in this list will influence what your life can become: lists help you to take decisions and to visualise your future. In this sense, they are our guides. Equally, they allow us to take different options into account. Making a list of your dreams for the future will not only bring pleasure to your present self, but it will also allow you to identify the aspects of these dreams which are achievable.

Suggested lists:

The key backdrops to my life (houses, schools, neighbourhoods, friendship groups… these headings will inspire a lot of memories)

My hobbies

My loves

My career.

Lists as self-portraits

'I am trapped between the beauty of June and the talent of Henry. I am drawn to both, in different ways. One part of me to each; the writer in me is drawn to Henry. June gives me a taste of danger. I must choose between them but I cannot.'

Anaïs Nin, *Diaries*

This is what Anaïs Nin wrote in her diary, after she had sketched both her lovers. One part of Anaïs wanted to be June, the other Henry. By analysing these competing impulses, Anaïs was eventually capable of reconciling them, and shining a light on her own identity as a writer and a woman. Making a list of the qualities you admire in a person allows you to decode what draws you to that person. And to discover who you would like to be... and who you would prefer not to be. The flaws we notice in others are often flaws we fear we may have; the qualities we notice in others are often qualities we would like to have. The choices we make – in terms of the people we spend time with, and the people we avoid or ignore – are therefore often a projection of who we are. These people represent and satisfy different facets of our personalities. And this explains why we can be drawn to very different types of people.

Sketch the portraits of people dear to you, then write down what they have brought to your life and how you change in their company. Every person we love teaches us to look at and appreciate the world through their eyes.

Suggested lists:

My best friends – who they are and what I like about them

My friends from my teenage years – the things we would do
together

The loves of my life – what attracted me to these people

The teachers who influenced me the most

The members of my family I am closest to

Strangers with whom I have had intense connections, whether
for hours or just minutes

People with very strong personalities who have influenced me

Characters in novels, fairy tales and films that have really
stayed with me.

Archetypes

Whenever you embark on an act of introspection, you must take dreams and the subconscious into account. And lists can be the ideal way of accessing that realm. Symbols and archetypes weave their way through our backstories. But how do we define these archetypes?

Most people think that if they defined themselves by archetypes, they would be as imprisoned as a butterfly in a jar. But we must abandon this belief. Adopting an archetype isn't the same as labelling yourself. In fact, it's the opposite. Archetypes are models, templates, images which guide us as we travel through our lives. Realising our true nature, and allowing it to hatch and flourish, is part of the beauty of living on a higher plane. We become the hero or heroine in a saga of mystical proportions. Indian sadhus do everything they can to imitate their gods, physically and spiritually, in order to get close to them. And, in a sense, these gods are their archetypes.

Carl Jung was convinced that archetypes were inhabited memories, concentrations of psychic energy represented by universal symbols and visible in myths and dreams. All of us, he claimed, had at least one archetype asleep in us, ready to be awakened by certain circumstances. According to Jung, what you do in life is a representation, either on a grand scale or a smaller scale, of the combination of your archetypes.

Ulysses, Mary Magdalene, Robinson Crusoe... who did you dream of when you were a child? Who were your heroes, your gods, your idols? Which books, which films, which fairy tales left the greatest mark on you? These archetypes are now part of you, so it is necessary to recognise them and take them into account when you consider who you are or would like to be. Living according to archetypes does not indicate a lack of personality or originality. We would not be the people we are if we had spent our youth on a desert island. What is interesting is why we have adopted, submitted to, kept or indeed rejected certain archetypes. This is what makes us individuals.

Let's try to discover these archetypes; this way we will be better able to recognise the extent to which a person – a hero, a saint, a writer, a character in a novel or a film – has inspired or even transformed us.

Suggested lists:

My heroes and heroines

My favourite books and films

My personal archetype for happiness

The objects which would fill an altar that reflected the centre
of my being

What my archetype(s) say to me

What my archetype(s) say through me

Things I would ask my archetype if I felt lost

What my archetypes do

What my archetypes think.

Dreams and nightmares

'How good it is to believe in the Loch Ness Monster, to feel a
frisson at these aquatic mysteries, which embody the sacred.'

Jean-Yves Renault, *Heal by Writing*

This is a very simple exercise. Under the heading 'My dreams', write down what you dreamt and date the entry. If applicable, write down the events which caused these dreams. Do the same with your nightmares. Detail the images succinctly and carefully. This will allow you not only to create order from the apparent chaos, but also to distil your dreams into a sort of poetry.

In this way, you can impose order on the images and unpack their contradictions. Once you have found a way of allowing the contradictory sentiments to exist in harmony, you can transform negative energies into a kind of creative expression. To turn a nightmare into a poem, all you need is a title. If you woke up before the nightmare finished, come up with a happy ending.

I dream that you are close to me
People came to save me
They laugh, they talk loudly, I am afraid.

I wake up. I write the dream down. Then I write two lines underneath:

But I know that you would not have let me go
You would have chased them away.

My wildest dreams and desires

'Life moves into the gaps between what is complete.'

Vladimir Jankélévitch

Who among us does not hope to wake up one day and realise a dream has come true? If you have always been too wise or sensible for this sort of thing, why don't you write down a list of all the crazy things you'd like to do? It's never too late to take a walk on the wild side, and to do so without worrying about looking eccentric or mad. Sometimes it is necessary to throw off the straitjacket of reason; to explore the unknown.

When you are writing this list, stop thinking and switch off the rational part of your brain. Let the words, images and dreams come of their own accord. Remember, there is more to you than the reasonable image you project to the world and which the world reflects back at you. You are at least one other person, and this other self is as hidden from you as it is from other people. What is stopping you from allowing these other selves to emerge when you are drawing or writing your self-portrait? On this list, anything goes: going round the world on a bicycle, living as a hermit in the mountains of China, working in a bar in Manhattan, doing up a crumbling country pile in Auvergne. It is only by writing a list of all these different selves – including the craziest, most extreme selves – that you will discover who you really are. And why you have made – or indeed avoided – certain life choices.

Some of these desires (or dreams) will be stronger than others.

But even if they are nothing but flights of fancy, they are still concrete manifestations of our minds. And sometimes it is these dreams which generate the most powerful impulses. Even when they do not see the light of day, they refuse to leave us in peace (at least some of them). In any introspective work, it is necessary to write down these dreams, because they are very much part of us; they allow us to look to the future with enthusiasm and optimism. To stop dreaming, to stop desiring, is to die.

Suggested lists:
The crazy things I'd like to do
The person I would like to be
The lives I would like to lead
Things which let me throw off the straitjacket of reason.

The irrational world and me

'He who can no longer pause to wonder and stand rapt in awe, is as good as dead.'

Albert Einstein

The very fact of being alive makes metaphysicists of all of us – we have all, at some point, witnessed strange events: coincidences, premonitions, mysteries… These phenomena, however inexplicable they may be, are also part of our reality. Paying attention to them enriches our reality and adds a new dimension to it. We all believe, deep inside ourselves, that the world is not necessarily as it appears, and sometimes all it would take is for a veil to be lifted for one reality to become another.

Suggested lists (dating these entries will allow you to cross-check and see patterns emerging):

Strange phenomena in my life

Coincidences

Intuitions

Premonitions

Fortuitous things

Tarot readings, Yijing readings

Visits to the fortune teller

Predictions.

The magical fallout of lists

*'The most intense things happen to us before we realise they
are happening. And by the time we begin to open our eyes to
what is visible, we have been connected to what was invisible
for a very long time.'*

Gabriele D'Annunzio, *Nocturne*

'And the word became flesh'… Let us not forget that words can create. They can change the reality of our lives. Humans have always used words to determine their lives and evolution. Prayers, invocations, incantations, words with special powers, mantras… the energy of words is recognised throughout the world.

Writing down your dreams – even seemingly impossible dreams – may lead to a strange phenomenon: they may come true. Consider the times when things have happened at the exact moment you really wanted them to happen. Things you thought you could not do, but then you wrote them down and they happened. This is how the written word works its magic. But in fact it isn't magic: the phenomenon can be explained. Once you give shape to an idea, you inscribe it into reality. So our subconscious comes into its own; it pushes us to act in accordance with this wish. If, for example, you commit to paper the fact you have always dreamt of visiting Ha Long Bay, you are more likely to follow through than if you had left the thought to simply trail in your mind. When a dream is written down, it becomes a plan, and the more it becomes a plan, the more likely it is to come true. Make a file called Ha Long Bay, read up on the prices and see what happens… (Perhaps, unconsciously, you will begin making savings by not buying things you don't need, with a view to realising this dream.)

Make a list of your wishes – date them and keep them. Don't worry if they contradict each other. All you need to do is believe in the unthinkable, the unimaginable, in mysteries and miracles. Lists of wishes have more potential to change your life than you may think. Every word conceals a certain energy. When we commit our desires to paper, we accord more importance to them; we cherish them. Our words are the cement, and our dreams are the bricks. Once a decision is written down, it becomes only a matter of time before it is put into action. Be as precise as possible. The more you specify your desire, the more closely you describe it, the more you call it by its proper name, the more chance this desire will have of becoming reality. Come back to this list often.

I once knew a young man who dreamt of owning a Ferrari. For years he bought things at car boot sales and found things in bins, then resold them in Tokyo's flea markets, saving every last yen. One happy day, he was behind the wheel of his supercar.

But the magical consequences of lists are not limited to material things. Writing down emotional desires can be the first step towards their realisation. The Japanese are convinced of this. On the seventh day of the seventh month (7 July), for the festival of Tanabata (according to legend, every seven years two separated lovers cross the rivers of the sky to reunite), people go to temple and hang prayers on the trees in the courtyard. These prayers take the form of lists. People write, for example, that they wish a past love would remember them or come back to them. In Japan people say you should never fear something which you don't want to happen. And you certainly shouldn't write down your fears. If you do not want your lover to cheat on you, the most important thing is not to imagine your lover cheating on you. If you fear he may cheat on you, he will cheat on you.

It is therefore wise only to write down what you want to happen, not what you don't want to happen, because to write is to change the course of events.

Some temples even give out books of edible paper (almost like thin Communion wafer) and on each page the same wish is printed. Swallowing a page every day, and focusing on what it says, will make this wish come true. It is for each of us to judge where the line lies between charlatanism on the one hand and, on the other, a belief in the mystery and force of thought. Personally, I think it is better to believe in mystery than to close yourself off from the possibility of belief, to live in a prison of reason. Ask yourself: what do we have to lose by believing in the mysteries of the universe?

My dearest wishes:

What I would like to do one day
What I would like to become one day
What I would like to see happen.

3

As time goes by

Talk about your memories so you don't lose them

'Reiko had never kept a diary, and found himself unable to experience the pleasure of reading and rereading the happiness he had felt these last few months.'

Yukio Mishima, *Patriotism*

Memory brings order to thought. Memory helps us to control our environment and, quite simply, to live. Even remembering small things – a date, the name of a plant, where you left your keys – gives us a little frisson of satisfaction. Like a muscle, memory needs to be exercised. The act of making lists – searching for forgotten memories, making the effort to collect different types of information, comparing and choosing between them – strengthens this muscle. Without memory, what would become of our imagination? By writing down your memories, you take the burden off your brain and allow space for new memories to form. The overall effect is very revitalising.

But does memory grow old?

People say that an idle mind grows 'rusty' after the age of twenty – or forty (though I am surprised the mind functions as well as it does!). But it has been observed that elderly people who have kept their minds active – and remained open to the world – do not lose their memories.

Memory works by a process of connection and association: the fewer the elements already stored, the less chance there is that new elements can be registered and linked to existing elements. Conversely, the more knowledge a person possesses, the greater their ability to accumulate and manipulate new information. Memories breed memories. The more a person speaks a foreign language, the easier it becomes for them to acquire another. It's the snowball effect.

The Canadian novelist Nancy Huston has lived in France for decades. She explains that long-term expatriates, who do not have the opportunity to discuss memories of a shared past with those close to them, tire of relating experiences which mean nothing to those around them and end up keeping these memories inside themselves, where they wither and die.

Reconnecting with your childhood friends and talking about the past, refreshing your notes, your photos, are necessary activities so that you don't let a part of yourself die.

You must cultivate the garden of memory, and refresh your good memories in the same way you would water a flower. Otherwise they may disappear completely. The advantages of reactivating your memories by writing them down are immense. Memory is like a film. Conversations, feelings, sensations: all the things you carry inside yourself should be as accessible as a recording. You should be able to say: 'Rewind', 'fast forward' – everything could or might be there! Lists are by their very nature elliptical; they are a pure function of memory, unlike descriptions. And they give us the option of 'revising' these memories whenever we want to.

Suggested lists:

Proverbs

Maxims.

Lists, analogies and regroupings

A list can give us objectives. But in order to gain understanding, we need to bring our subjectivity to the table. Writing lists brings order to disparate elements by forcing us to group them under headings. But it is only when we reread our lists that resonances can emerge, as well as the emotions which link the disparate elements. By associating names, people and memories, you will discover what you have liked and disliked all along, without having become consciously aware of it.

Some people I knew in my childhood – like my neighbour Mme Légaret or my Aunt Louise Huguette; then later, in my reading of *The Private Papers of Henry Ryecroft* by George Gissing – made me realise why I like carefully designed small interiors, where everything is tranquil and in its place, methodically tidied, cleaned and respected. So many elements of our childhoods and life experiences are catalysts for how our lives turn out, for our tendencies and our ways of thinking.

Our memories are not linear. They do not obey chronology. They come back to us in loops, by association and regrouping.

How all this information is stored is still not understood by modern science (memories may even be stored in each individual cell of our bodies). But what is certain is that they are not stored in chronological order. And that is where the logic of lists – as opposed to the linear chronology of a diary – comes in handy.

When you describe the places you have visited, or what happened in the course of an evening with friends, you don't begin by 'rereading' these memories. You draw the main protagonists in broad brush strokes, the place, the main events, and only then do you add descriptive detail. Think, for example, of a series of images which evoke 'youth' for you – a word which can call up all sorts of memories. When you remember such-and-such an event, you don't do so in phrases. Names, images, feelings… this is what comes to mind first. These memories do not arrive in complete sentences with a subject, a verb and an object, because this is not how memories come to be stored. If you described a meal by saying, 'The starter was fresh seafood, it was excellent, then a roast with vegetables from the garden, prepared by the great-aunt, then…' the person listening to you would not grasp the meaning so clearly as if you'd said 'seafood, roast meat with potatoes, salad, cheese then lemon tart'. Ninety per cent of the words used will not be stored in the memory, and will disappear in a few seconds between the key words which the brain picks up on, thus weakening our ability to see connections between ideas and associating them.

Our brains don't process language in a linear way, or in the form of lists for that matter. They integrate key concepts and add elements to other elements. The process is a chain reaction. So the principle of 'Japanese steps' involves regrouping everything you want to remember under one heading, in a 'holographic' way. In the middle of a large sheet of paper, write down an overarching theme (holidays, for example), and then allow other elements to attach themselves. Then, with the help of key words, you will be able to give your memories structure, to write down the elements in the form of a list, and in the order which is best for you. You will be surprised by how little time this takes. And your brain will be open to all sorts of creativity…

Je me souviens, by Georges Perec

Je me souviens by Georges Perec is a list of 480 memories, not only the personal memories of the author but also snippets of a shared past; lots of small, everyday things which everyone who lived in that particular era would have experienced and then perhaps forgotten. Things too trivial to be written down or memorised, but which recur in conversations, small memories still intact: things learnt at school or heard on the radio, scandals, turns of speech, fashions, things which may be trivial but still evoke a certain nostalgia years later. (I have chosen the following excerpts because they remind me of the first decade of my life: school trips to the cinema, the small dog in the window which barked at my mother, the milk which I would fetch from the neighbouring farm with my grandmother…)

I remember

Doctor Schweizer

I remember

Newsreels at the cinema

I remember

That we used to go and fetch milk in a battered tin can

I remember

How much for that doggie in the window, the lovely little black
and white dog.

Artists, intellectuals, architects, poets, parents… every human feels the instinct to leave a part of themselves to posterity. But the best mark to leave on the world is a parcel of light, of happiness, of beauty. No life is lived in vain. Lists prove this to us even if one day they are, like us, reduced to a fistful of ash.

PART THREE

LISTS FOR SELF-CARE

1

Lists are wonderful tools for self-analysis

Write to correct your own blindness

'When I write in my notebooks, I write myself.
But I don't write my whole self.'

Paul Valéry, *Cahiers*

Every day, life is a series of choices. Describing these, by writing them down, is a form of therapy – admittedly a taxing one, some-times – but a therapy nonetheless. And one that can help restore our balance. Writing connects us to ourselves. It allows us to deepen ourselves, to make new choices. Writing invites us to respect ourselves more, to pinpoint our flaws, our failings and defi-ciencies. It helps us to correct our blind spots, to wake from mental slumber, to become fully aware of what is happening around us and within us.

Writing is thinking twice

'Thoughts and words create our future experiences.'

Louise Hay, *You Can Heal Your Life*

One evening I was watching a Japanese television programme, which said that the goal of reading and writing was to live better. That short phrase stayed with me. If reading and thinking are indispensable to our evolution, then writing helps us to clarify and crystallise our thoughts. For example, by writing notes on the books you read, you will make the ideas which grab your attention your own; they will stay with you profoundly, and certainly far more than if you'd simply put the book down once you'd turned the last page. Taking notes forces us to take the time to reflect. We can and must question ourselves constantly, and refine our ways of thinking.

Writing facilitates thought in many ways. It gives form to our feelings, our reflections, our annotations, our quotations, our poetic impulses, our plans... Our writings are like a storeroom. The ideas in this storeroom may be provisional, they may be in flux. But however incomplete they may be, they contain a vast array of 'drafts' of ourselves. If you take these drafts and reorder them in the form of lists (for example, lists of your fears, of the things which make you angry, of your responsibilities), you can subject them to analysis. Lists will be easier to analyse than free writing. By writing lists, you will organise your mind in a tangible way; you will realise your own identity. By seeing yourself on paper, you will take a step back. This is how you can stop repeating self-destructive behaviour, once and for all. This is a feedback loop.

By compiling a report not only of your weaknesses, but also of your fears, angers and doubts, you will realise what is happening within you, and you will learn to accept those things – then correct and change them if you think that is a good idea. Or change nothing, if you can live with the consequences of your actions (with a clear conscience). Your faults and weaknesses will then become part of your identity, consciously acknowledged as such. If you realise you are disturbed by how you act, these moments of recognition will give you the means with which to identify what you are doing wrong.

Then begin a list of everything you have noticed about yourself. Include your good points and your flaws. Include things you have said or done in moments of anger or conflict, things which strike you as out of character. But whatever you do, don't judge the person you were in that moment. Your lists reveal the person under the masks you wear in the world. Love that person, that person only you can really know. Accept that person. Don't be harsh on that person. Look at that person with the heart of an adult, with compassion and love. In the cold light of day, you will see things more objectively than your past self could have done in the moment. Mistakes, hesitations, moments of blindness – all these things serve a purpose. Like nature, we are in a constant state of flux. We don't have to become an ideal being. No one is asking us to be a specific person. Human nature is inherently contradictory. But to be mature, it is necessary to be aware of these contradictions, and to try to live as harmoniously as possible with all the selves which make up your person.

127

Write to get your bearings

'Seize time in the mesh of the phrase.'

Patrick Modiano

Why write about your life? Why write an account of yourself? Surely we know our lives well enough…

But it is worth trying this. Writing down the trajectory of our lives gives us the bigger picture. It allows us to understand that our lives have been defined by the principle of cause and effect. And we can better realise how, without even having been aware of it, we have indeed been the authors of our own lives. We will understand that the whims of our lives, ultimately, owe nothing to chance. And that perhaps, also, we have been manipulated by the system we live in.

We grow up in a world which tries to convince us that we are all ill and stressed, behind the times and behind on what we need to do. We are constantly being told that we need to change, to adopt one philosophy or another, one brand of politics or another, a religion, a mode of thinking. We no longer know what to think. We no longer know at which altar to worship, which way of living to adopt. But the answers to the questions we ask ourselves are already in us. Writing is not only a form of reclaiming what the world owes us, it is also a way of reclaiming ourselves. It is one of the ways in which we can reconnect with ourselves, and also with a higher level of our being. We need to rediscover a sense of unity, to recentre ourselves.

In difficult times – in times of tension and crisis, whether personal or public – the most important thing is to remain centred and to keep your calm. Not to allow yourself to be influenced or swept away by circumstances, however dramatic these may be, or by negative energies or emotions.

This is by no means an easy task. But in trying times, turn inward. This is where the most reliable, trusty help can be found. And this is where you can derive benefits from the habit of writing regularly about yourself. Writing brings clarity and passion to the act of living; it frees us from the shackles of reason, of everyday life, of other people. Writing helps us to live more vigorously and more optimistically; to find strength and balance; to find our own bearings and reconnect with our intuition. Words accompany us on our journey. They also make sure we don't stray from our path. Sometimes just a few phrases will be enough to remind us that we exist.

The structure of a list doesn't only represent order. It creates order. It's not a case of waking up one day and thinking you need to 'find' yourself. It is a case of always being aware, and increasing your awareness.

To write is to harvest your existence. Write down what you are doing, what you are feeling, what you are dreaming of. To write is to rediscover your own codes, to find the keys to your memory, to document any number of little things which will in turn breathe life into your thoughts, your sense of poetry, your own philosophy. It is a path towards understanding yourself, to understanding others, and to understanding the world. These thousands of little writings will become your personal bible, and also your guide to yourself. They will reflect the world which we have created, and the world which we continue to create. Only this book can allow us to rediscover the harmony, the unity, the sense of self which we have lost growing up in an increasingly superficial, hectic world. Because lists are 'fixed', they allow us to find our bearings. They bring us a sense of unity, and enable us to discover a way of life and a way of thinking which are unique to who we are.

Suggested lists:

My career plans

My travel plans

The ambitions I have for my home

The people I can rely on

What belongs to me and only me (knowledge, material goods)

What the most powerful experiences of my life have taught me

The people I respect for their sense and stability

The safety nets I have in place in case I lose my job, my
partner, my lover

My psychological supports (a list of quotes I can call on)

What I feel in certain situations

Experiences I would never like to repeat.

Write to take charge of yourself

'Before trying to learn anything complicated, learn to read love letters sent by the wind, the rain, the snow and the moon.'

Ikkyu, a Japanese tea master

In ancient cultures, people had to take charge of their thoughts and actions. In Confucian China and Spartan antiquity, among the Romans, the pilgrim founders of New England or British aristocrats in Victorian times, everyone had a duty to keep strict control of their emotions. If you bemoaned your fate or acted according to your own instincts, you would forfeit your right to be part of that particular society.

Each and every one of us is capable of controlling our emotions and, with that in mind, of working on our thoughts, feelings and motivations. In doing so, we may change their nature. But again, the first step towards doing so is to see things as they are – and also as they could and should be.

Writing an account of your life, in the form of lists, allows you to take responsibility for your own life, and that will, ultimately, make you more grown up.

What do we need to do? We need to write, we need to question ourselves, we need to reflect on ourselves. We need to always remember that the path to inner peace and happiness is working on ourselves. It is up to us – and only us – to find our balance and, with that, our health. We must take ourselves in hand and learn to use the resources we carry within us. But we must also give ourselves enough time, and we must not fall for quick fixes which, in the long run, only complicate our problems and make them even more difficult to solve. No one can tell us the meaning of life, or our karma, or the challenges we need to face in order to mature and evolve.

Writing is one of the best ways of solving your problems on your own. What is going on in our heads and in our hearts? And why? The things which weigh us down are the choices *we* make. So what can we do to feel lighter, to feel more alive? We are constantly being called upon to change, to readjust our priorities. But isn't that the stuff of life?

Suggested lists on responsibilities:

Things I am responsible for

Things I am not responsible for

Things I no longer want to be responsible for.

Suggested lists on burdens:

Things I can dispense with to make me feel more alive

Things I can dispense with to make me feel lighter

The things which weigh down my head – and why

The things which weight down my heart – and why.

Write to articulate things better

'An oyster
Is a little house
For a creature which dwells in seaweed.'

Haiku by Ichu

Lists force us to define and to clarify. They invite us to be more perceptive, and to expand our consciousness by reflecting, exploring and questioning ourselves. They allow us to become more decisive and more precise.

Take a moment, for example, to describe the table you are sitting at: what is its structure, its form, its attributes? What does it make you think of? Writing down your thoughts is a way of capturing them, and of making them real. Otherwise they will remain vague. But it is also necessary to articulate your thoughts, to order them and, in that way, to control and possess them. When we articulate a thought or name a thing, it becomes ours.

Using lists to re-edit your memories or your writing breeds integrity and rigour. In the absence of long paragraphs you cannot 'pad out' the facts – you have to confront them. You can no longer lie to yourself, or hide the facts from yourself, by cloaking them in different interpretations. With lists, you can even express the inexpressible. If you can't quite articulate what you are feeling, make a list with two columns where, in the left-hand column, you describe the feeling with the words currently available to you. Then wait, for weeks even. At the moment you least expect it, the right expression will come to you. Note it down in the right hand column.

Suggested lists:

My 'personal collection' of words and expressions relating to emotion

The people or situations which inspire in me a feeling that I can't put into words right now

Vocabulary which might be useful to me

Images corresponding to some of my feelings.

Write to be lucid

'I write down the date, the place and the time; and I begin to document – I like that word – a multitude of little things, of thoughts, of things I felt yesterday and things I feel today. I report on time; I report on my life [...] I'm fascinated by traces [...] of the past, of lived experience, of feeling [...] feeding my knowledge of myself, of others, of the world.'

Philippe Lejeune, *On Diary*

The act of putting pen to paper, and the concision and choices involved (the style, the words, the images and analogies, the layout of phrases), makes us more exact with ourselves. And that in turn sheds, with each iteration, more light on who we really are.

Mapping out what makes you happy and what makes you unhappy, identifying the status quo of your life, identifying when you are ready to snap... All these things incite you to change. The therapeutic quality of writing makes us realise that we are in fact the authors of our own lives. And this in turn helps us to rewrite our lives, and live them in a way which is more proactive and more personally satisfying.

The act of writing helps us not only to master our minds, but also to lighten our mental load. The emotional weight of our childhood memories plays a large role in the adults we become, and in the way our minds work. So it is necessary to be fully aware of our own histories. The process of recalling the past can be a very positive one. Isn't this why we take photos, collect keepsakes, turn our homes into family museums?

Keeping a good record of the past can improve our quality of life immeasurably. It liberates us from the tyranny of the past and allows us to recall our memories at will. This way we can curate our pasts. We can select pleasing and significant memories, remodel or 'create' a past with which we can better face the future. It is only in understanding our past that we can build our future in a psychologically healthy way, that we can understand our lives and the mistakes we may potentially make.

What starts out as a simple tally of your achievements and failures will become a story which has meaning, and which you can consider your own.

Independently analysing your past is not only possible, it is also extremely gratifying: you will feel like the master of your own destiny; you will feel happy or, at the very least, serene. You will not be dependent on anyone else, and that will give you a huge amount of energy. The most important thing when writing introspective lists like these is to be completely honest and not lie to yourself. Force yourself to always tell the truth, no matter how hard this is, no matter how much it hurts. Don't be afraid to write down distressing things, things you would rather hide. Because otherwise progress is impossible.

You can write lists in two columns. For example, 'For' and 'Against', or 'Events as they happened' and 'How I experienced those events', with the facts on the left and your interpretations on the right. Putting facts on paper, in black and white, is like shining a torch into your mental fog.

Suggested lists:

I would say this if it weren't too dangerous…

I'm not ready yet, but one day I would…

My failings and my limits

My weaknesses

My fears

My worries

The images which go through my head most often

The experiences which have influenced, inspired, changed or
moulded my life.

2

Stop being a victim of your emotions

Take stock of your emotions

'Things which move me profoundly:
The drops of late autumn dew which glisten like pearls on the
reeds in the garden
Waking at sunrise
A mountain village under snow.'

Sei Shonagon, *The Pillow Book*

Fear, frustration, anger and worry are mental energies which can be dominated or suppressed. But first of all, you have to identify these feelings. Then, as Zen says, the transformation will come from within. It's just like gardening: extract the weeds and the stones, make cuttings, trim, prune, water the ground so it is ready to push forth new life. The same principle applies to our lives: we must begin by trimming back what is preventing us from developing, and to do that, we must identify exactly what is holding us back.

We go through our lives mostly unaware of our own strength. But the more we work on our lives, and the more we accept our responsibilities, the wider our horizons will become. We make lists to unburden ourselves. Making lists is a way of moving on. A way of sorting, extracting, sweeping, discarding and purging.

In Western culture, the majority of people think that emotions are the spice of life, and would not renounce them for anything. They think life would be nothing without emotions. But they also know that emotions make them suffer, and weaken them. Experiencing emotion and feeling joy are not the same thing. In order to reach serenity we must change, but also accept the things we are not in a position to change and turn our backs on them. If we are humbled and poised, and if we let these qualities guide and counsel us, we can make a huge difference to our quality of life.

The only way to really *know* what disturbs us (our resentments, frustrations, jealousies and irritations) is to understand where these feelings come from and the needs they are responding to. We do not have to try to eliminate negative feelings; we simply need to be fully aware of them. That way, the next time these feelings surface, we will be better placed not to react impulsively. Negative thoughts drain us. I have often noticed that I have caught a cold after an upset (an argument, an annoyance, a failure…). Some doctors believe that worrying creates a chemical imbalance in the brain, which acidifies the blood, and this in turn affects our immune system.

Stop trying to be right all the time. Find a place for compassion. This will really help you to achieve a sense of distance and detachment, and to act as though your problems don't have such a grip on you. If we manage to hope and dream without burying ourselves in emotion, we will be an awful lot happier.

A LIST OF THINGS WHICH MAKE ME TOO EMOTIONAL (AND SO EXHAUST ME):

Talking about myself too much
Conflicts with those close to me
Unstable relationships
Criticising or trying to change other people
Things over which I have no control but which I try to change
A bad night's sleep
Tiredness due to noise
Alcohol.

Suggested lists:

The things which worry me the most
The emotions which dictate my life
Troubling situations I have to face
What these situations provoke in me
The ideal solution
The compromise solution.

The balance sheet of your thoughts

'Candlelight

A magnificent night

Frogs croak.'

Haiku by Kobayashi Issa

In *The New Diary*, Tristine Rainer recommends writing as a sort of catharsis. She recommends a type of free writing where we can pour out our worries, fears and confusions. Rainer is an expert on diary- and memoir -writing, and on the therapeutic effects of these activities. She explains that putting your pain to bed by writing it down allows you to recover your emotional balance, and can save you from self-destruction. In California, people say that writing one page by hand, for half an hour every morning – free-writing, without stopping – has a better effect on your appearance than a face mask. When you feel better in yourself, it shows.

Julia Cameron, in her book *The Artist's Way*, recommends writing three pages every morning. She calls these Morning Pages. The point of this exercise is to express all the things within us which we have a tendency to suppress. 'These pages are not an exercise in style or in literary creation, nor an exercise in diary-keeping, although they can and sometimes do become those things. Do not write with a reader in mind, write for no one, not even yourself.' Cameron recommends not reading your writing back immediately, leaving at least five weeks before doing so. The point of this exercise isn't to satisfy the ego; on the contrary, the point is to purge yourself of it, and of what pollutes your ego on a subconscious level.

Morning Pages are also an unbeatable way of developing your creativity, and rousing the artist which lies dormant in us all. Empty your head. Relax, and simply wait until something arrives under the nib of your pen. Follow the example of the surrealists, who championed auto-writing. Write without seeking to control your words, and don't worry whether they make sense or not. Allow your hand to move as quickly as possible so your mind doesn't have the time to self-censor. That way, you will realise how you go from a childlike way of thinking to a mature one, simply by writing on the page, and this way you will become aware of how your mind works.

But then process everything you have written down, and do this in the form of lists. In my opinion, this next step is just as important to achieve those famous cathartic moments. Go back to these moments and make a neat, clear list of the ideas which went through your head. A torrent of words will not bring you much. The most important things are what the torrent hides.

Suggested lists (all the entries in these lists should be no longer than one line):
The type of thoughts which cross my mind in the course of a day
The thoughts I have as I am falling asleep
The thoughts I have when I can't get to sleep
The thoughts I have when I am angry, frustrated or anxious
The thoughts I have when I am feeling on great form or in places which I particularly like.

Writing as an outlet for excess emotion

'Expressing myself was necessary to save my identity and my self-respect, and to fight depression.'

Philippe Lejeune, *On Diary*

Lists are an ideal way of letting off steam, in the same way some people do on a therapist's couch. They allow you to organise different things under one heading, to combine them, to accumulate information, signs and details, to become conscious of how things really are, and to evolve. They allow you to rid yourself of the superfluous, so that only the essential remains. This way, you will know how to surf the waves of life, not only without drowning, but with balance and pleasure.

In order to distance yourself from negativity, to extract it from yourself, you need no one but yourself. Writing will free you from what is hurting or thwarting you. Having confined your anger, worries and pain to paper, you will feel emptied, with weary hands but a light, refreshed head. What a liberating tool lists are!

Writing lists allows you to free yourself from harmful emotions without having to unleash an avalanche of personal, intimate information on those around you (we often regret having said too much, realising afterwards that we did so not to bring something to others, but to make ourselves feel better).

Lists help you to exercise restraint and self-control… and to retain your mystery. They are our mirror, our confidant, our guide, our therapist, our secret garden. They help to shoulder the weight of our sufferings, or a difficult past.

Examine the emotions you feel you have no control over, the emotions which are causing your current problems. Simply observe them. Now remove the label 'bad' and accept these emotions for what they are. Whether they are bad or good, they are only emotions. Nothing more and nothing less. Instead of labelling them, view them as energies and write them down. You have become an observer. All you are doing is viewing your emotions as energies. Your feelings of sadness, anxiety or fear will dissipate as soon as you have observed them and written them down. Writing them down in black and white allows you to externalise them. And in doing so, you remove the power they have over you. By becoming less emotionally attached to your problems, you will make it easier for solutions to present themselves. By observing your pain, you can divorce yourself from it. Every experience can teach you something. Say thank you for the lesson and move on.

Suggested lists:

What I am feeling at this exact moment
The emotions I most often fall prey to
The emotions which control me
The people who have wronged me
The events which have hurt me
The events which have caused me to let myself go
The lessons I have learnt from situations where I have seen
     myself as the victim
Strategies for no longer being a victim of my emotions.

What we talk about when we talk about love

'Adopting another person's way of understanding is the best way of getting to know their world.'

Richard Bandler, an eminent American neurologist

Writing helps us to better understand what has happened between us and other people, how we have been loved or rejected, supported or suffocated… It gives us the feeling of existing, of telling our own story and working out the chain of events which have made us who we are. Do not get caught up in conflicts you cannot solve. Rise above them. The challenges which you devote time and mental energy to should be surmountable ones. If you do not write, you will lose track of who you are. Don't stick your head in the sand and think that what is missing from your life is other people.

Talk to yourself. For example, when you think of a romantic partner who you are not happy with, write: 'She has many qualities, but she doesn't really know you'/'You think you love him but your love has distorted your perception. He isn't who you dream he is. He is simply the person he is now, and his behaviour towards women stems from his own problems – it has nothing to do with you. He is the only person who can solve his own problems. You need to focus on your own goals.' You can also write a list of what the relationship has taught you. This type of list will make you discover a new side to the other person, a side you hadn't realised existed.

Finally, try to become more independent. You could write a list called 'My declaration of independence' in which you write exactly what you do and don't want.

Suggested lists:

The loves of my life

The reasons I loved those people

The reasons we split

Unresolved dilemmas and situations in my life

What I can learn from each of these experiences

The positive aspects of these experiences

Silences and things left unsaid (my own and others')

My 'declaration of independence'.

When you just can't stop thinking about someone

'I would love to say to someone
Look at those fireflies
Yet I am quite alone.'

Haiku by Taïgi

Sometimes we just can't stop thinking about someone, even when we are busy working and supposed to be thinking about something else. We think about what we would like to say to him, what we want from her… Making a list of your thoughts will force you to become fully conscious of them, and then you will have more control over them. By writing down these thoughts, you will think less about the other person and more about yourself. You will stop living your life at half capacity, you will stop thinking only half your thoughts, you will stop being only half yourself.

You can also write 'phantom' letters, which you will never send. If you make a list of things you would like to say to that person, you will change your mindset without ever having to say these things out loud. You will have more clarity, you will know more keenly what you want and don't want, and you will be in a position to say no to certain things without explanations or tears.

You can also make a list of what isn't satisfying you in a relationship, or what is making you uncomfortable. This exercise can also help you rediscover your own values and act accordingly. And, above all, it will help you do everything you can to make sure that you are not reliant on anyone else, and only want things which you can achieve on your own.

Suggested lists:

Things I can achieve on my own

Things I can change in my life to make me independent (and, against this list, the means of achieving them)

Things I can't change in another person

Things which make me dependent on other people.

Don't see yourself as a victim

'May my love for you
Never become oppressive
Because I have chosen to
Love you, freely.'

A poem by Rabindranath Tagore

Even if you want to express your emotions as clearly as possible, avoid words which portray you as a victim. For example, don't say that you are angry, anxious, scared, ashamed, bored, confused, rejected, dispossessed, discontented, sad, tired, guilty, hostile, irrational, jealous, lazy, alone… Avoid words which imply that another person has made you feel something, like abused, abandoned, betrayed, cheated on, diminished, manipulated, misunderstood, overworked, rejected…

By using such words, you are giving other people power over your emotions. You will, in turn, attract people who provoke those feelings, and you will end up in a vicious circle. It is very difficult to be happy when you can't control your own emotions.

It is up to you to choose who you want to be. No one can make you feel things you don't want to feel. If you have decided to leave someone because they are bad for you, write down everything you don't like about that person, all your complaints, and don't leave anything out. Every detail will help; read and reread this list. Perhaps even carry this list around with you. Every time you're on the verge of 'cracking', read it back. Add things you've forgotten. Read it and reread it, to reinforce the choice you have made. If you want to leave them, take out this list every time you find yourself thinking about them.

Once we externalise our frustrations, they are no longer part of us and they can do us no harm. They will be imprisoned on paper, so to speak. By announcing them, we are denouncing them; they will lose their power over us. We will have the potential to master them. The things which worry us, the things which become unbearable, are the things which evade our understanding, which cannot be expressed, named or described. Diagnosing an illness is the first step towards treating it.

By realising that we are bogged down in emotions, we can get a better handle on our situation, and we are better able to escape it. In this way, lists become a survival mechanism.

Suggested lists:

What I don't like about this person

Things I don't like in this relationship

The needs I have which are not being satisfied

The qualities I have which my partner doesn't value

The things I will look for in my next relationship which I haven't had in this one

The next time I see this person I will say… (this will save you broken china – you will not say these things because you have written them down!)

My most frequent thoughts about him/her

My fears

My frustrations

My reproaches.

3

When nothing is going right...

Some words on your troubles

'When will you stop talking such nonsense?
(Then shouting insults in Latin or... in Japanese, which you
have learnt by heart)'

Fred Vargas, *A Little Treaty on Boredom*

When we want to let off steam, writing soothes us almost immediately. Writing gives us space, and allows us to calm down. It is the key to serenity and detachment. By committing to paper what stresses or irritates us, when reading it back, we distance ourselves from the causes of our anguish. As soon as we close our notebook, the problem is far away, imprisoned, named, easier to identify. It loses the interest it held. Hide the causes of your anger and stress on paper: then they will no longer control you. Offloading is the very best sleeping pill. Just try it! You can also stop focusing on your anger by making lists of little 'ridiculous' things. (For example, clothes which go together, what you would wear if you lost ten kilograms, places you'd like to go to on your own, adventures...)

Try to understand exactly what you want from life. Make your wishes as clear and detailed as possible. That will help spare you from things which are bad for you: stress and anger. If you can't manage to do this exercise, tell yourself that there are blockages in your head. Sometimes, the inability to write stems from being overwhelmed. It's as though too many thoughts and emotions are flooding in simultaneously, asking to be liberated. And so you get writer's block. In order to overcome this, make a list of the most important things that are going through your head. Keep it to one page. Then go through the entries one by one, trying to pinpoint which is bothering you the most. That will most likely be the thing which is blocking you.

By keeping a book of lists, you will learn how much your ability to relax depends on your ability to concentrate. Focus on the voice inside your head; forget that you are writing. When you are tired or blocked, stop for a moment and reread your list of 'visualisations'. This can be an excellent tool for calming down in ten minutes. Of course, what goes on this list is up to you, but here are some examples.

VISUALISATIONS TO HELP ME RELAX

Listen to the sounds of my body

Breathe deeply and slowly

Focus on a white light

Focus on the silence within me.

A LIST OF 'BALMS FOR YOUR SOUL' FOR WHEN YOU ARE ANGRY OR STRESSED

Spend a night in a small hotel

Go out to buy cigarettes and gin

Get my nails done or go to the hairdresser

Clear up and throw out useless, ugly things

Go for a brisk walk

Go to the cinema

Take a bath scented with rose water.

Suggested lists 'for the bin' – lists you write to be thrown out. (This technique helps to de-stress you, and prevents you from saying or doing things you can't take back. For example, sending a rash break-up letter, or hurling insults in moments of anger. We always feel better when we manage to get over our anger, while keeping our feelings to ourselves.)

Reasons why I am angry at the moment

What I would say if I bumped into [the person who is hurting me at the moment]

My favourite insults

A list of the types of reasons (real or imagined) for turning down an offer

Acts of revenge

What is irritating me at the moment

My resentments towards…

The state of my physical health when I'm angry

The state of my mental health when I'm angry

The things and people which have made me angry (date these entries)

What I want

What I don't want

Things which calm me down when I'm angry or stressed

Small lists of 'ridiculous' things which make me feel better

Balms for my soul.

Write down your fears and worries to push them away

The act of writing down your fears – even your most anodyne fears – will make you realise, as though by magic, that they are far less frightening once they are committed to paper (for example, the fear of having a certain illness, of having an accident, of losing someone close to you). You can keep a second column, 'Positive solutions', to ward off these fears. You don't need to write down a solution immediately. As soon as you record your fears, your subconscious will automatically try to find a solution, and that solution may present itself when you least expect it. You will find a way to master your fears, even your deepest ones. This is a method frequently used by psychoanalysts.

Because worries are worries, it is often difficult to identify and name them. But you can always make a list of the things you feel: where, when, in what context, as a result of what.

Suggested lists:
Things I am apprehensive about (with a second, positive
    solutions column)
My fears (two columns)
My anxieties (in terms of the things I feel)
The images which cross my mind most often
What I can do when I'm anxious
The lists I should reread when I feel anxious.

When you have the blues

*'Everyone experiences problems, disappointments
and frustrations. What shapes our lives is how we
respond to these obstacles.'*

Tony Robbins

Nothing is permanent. And nothing is useless. Every torment serves to perfect you, in the same way every journey does. Some people claim that lists – and, by extension, words – fix reality in place, and so they cannot reflect our true reality because we change with every moment, because nothing is permanent. This is the fundamental tenet of Buddhism. But there are moments in life when 'abstract' support simply will not do. Lists exist to take us back to reality. They serve as a tangible support not only when we question things, but also in our moments of sadness, melancholy, discouragement and blues; when we feel empty inside. They are there to remind us that the sky isn't always grey, that we don't always have to be on top form, that we need to allow these moments to pass. That they are inevitable but that they *will* pass.

Listing gives us energy. Leafing through our 'treasure trove' when we're feeling down or when we feel as though we have lost our bearings is an excellent way of feeling more dynamic. These lists remind us of the wonderful things we have experienced, the things we love and have loved, of plans which may seem impossible to realise today but which will probably be realised one day, if only we... In the same way we may try to recharge a dead battery by applying sparks, these lists are the sparks which can rescue us.

Making lists can console you, make you happy, change you, calm you, empty your mind, inspire you and open your heart and your head to deeper reflections. It can even help you to shake off depression.

To make lists is to reorder your life, and to become more deeply aware of things, events and situations. It is to transform your wounds into works of art. Life will continue to offer us all the good and beautiful things it has already offered us, even if these take a different form.

Rereading your list of 1,001 small pleasures (see Part Four) or your favourite haikus, is like opening your medicine cabinet and taking out the treatment for the malady you are experiencing at that moment. It immediately reconnects you with a feeling of well-being.

Your book of lists could just as easily be called 'My pharmacy for the mind'.

Apathy, anxiety and depression are often caused by repressed emotions (desire, jealousy, anger, fear, feelings of guilt), by overwork or by disorganisation. Make a list of what needs to be done, quickly and without thinking of your emotions, then choose one manageable thing on your list and do it immediately. Leave the house, go and see an exhibition or a film, repot your plants, wash your car. Get outside and immerse yourself in the flow of life. When you feel down, you tend to live in slow motion. You stop moving. You lack energy; you feel like a kite on a windless day.

Suggested lists:
Comforting things for difficult days

Everything you need to do

The things and people that energise me

Future plans (journeys, holidays, moving house or job)

Activities which immediately release me from torpor or apathy.

The principle of opposites

'Happiness is to unhappiness as life is to death.'

Simone de Beauvoir, interviewed in a documentary about herself and
Jean-Paul Sartre, directed by Madeleine Gobeil-Noël

Hope and despair. Sorrow and joy. Every thought has its opposite. Every depression contains its own antidote.

Make a list entitled 'The principle of opposites'. Rereading it in moments when you feel hollow will bring you comfort. We do not need much to live; hardly anything. If you discover what is good for you and stick to it, you will be fulfilled. You will know what to live for, and what to die for. Ask yourself, 'What is annoying me at the moment?', 'What am I hiding from myself?' Katherine Mansfield, the famous American short-story writer, often used these sorts of reflections in her diary, in order to work out what she really wanted.

She wrote: 'Now Katherine, what do you really mean by HEALTH?' And she replied: 'I mean the power to live a full, adult life, to inhale life, to be in close contact with what I love, with the wonders of the earth, the sea, the sun. And I want to work. On what? I want to work with my hands and my heart and my head. I want a garden, a small house, grass, animals, books, paintings, music. And to express all those things. To write!'

Suggested lists:

A list of the hundred things I love most in life and the hundred
things I love least

My best holiday memories, the mark they made on me; my
worst holiday memories
The people who like me and those who dislike me; the people I
like and those I dislike
What I'm finding enjoyable at the moment; what I'm finding
tedious.

Mourn certain things

'The act of living is constantly taking yourself apart and putting yourself back together again, changing state and shape, dying and being reborn.'

from The Great *Almanac of Japanese Poetry*

What does it mean to fail at life? Perhaps it means dwelling on memories instead of focusing on each new day; preferring stasis and rigidity to the growth of new life; holding onto old certainties instead of questioning ourselves.

If we wish to transform our lives into a fecund reality, we must look into our past dreams, with as much self-awareness as possible, and work out which are constructive and hold promise, and which are false friends, which entrap us.

This sort of exercise can be painful at the beginning. We always feel less at ease in a new belief system, regardless of how misguided our old one was.

We prefer to make our lives easy in the short term, even if it causes future suffering; in the same way we nearly always choose immediate gratification, even if that brings less pleasure in the future. To liberate yourself from the intimacies of your past you must relive it, 'go back inside yourself', and do so with all the intensity of the original emotion linked to that memory. It is far more difficult to renounce the things you have never had than the things you have. You can make a list of things you wish to renounce mentally (thoughts, ideas, religious convictions, and so on) and also physically (not only addictions to food, cigarettes, drugs, but also to certain types of situation or to superficial things).

Give your suffering meaning

'The deeper that sorrow carves into your being,
the more joy you can contain.'

Kahlil Gibran

The first step towards confronting your problems is not seeking to escape them. Trying to escape them lends them importance. Remember all the difficult things you have experienced and compile a list of them. This list will become a treasure trove of life knowledge, which will help you give meaning to your current suffering. Every experience is valuable in its own way. Writing this list is a way of never forgetting the wisdom we have gleaned from the trials of the past, from the mistakes we have made, from our patience, from our faults and our life experience as a whole. We gain strength, courage and self-confidence by focusing on every difficulty we have overcome, every fear we have tackled head-on. We can say to ourselves: 'I have already experienced this trial. I can stand what is to come.' Courage is a private victory, not a public one. Secret acts of courage breed other, secret acts of courage.

Be very particular about how you express yourself in this sort of list. The richer, the more beautiful your language, the easier it will be to sublimate your pain. A legitimate feeling of pride at how you have surmounted difficulties will reconcile you with yourself, and with your current suffering.

Suggested lists:

The difficulties I have overcome

My sufferings (left-hand column) and what they have taught
   me (right-hand column)

Brave things I have done

Brave things I now feel in a position to do

Poems, words, landscapes, music etc which express or soothe
   my pain

The things I grieve.

Self-love, self-respect, self-worth

'Perhaps there is only one real illness,
and that is not being yourself.'

Jean-Yves Renault, writing therapist

Rarely do we allow ourselves to… be ourselves. For that to happen, we must have breathing space, we must not feel under pressure. We must not feel burdened by the external world, by what Taoists call 'the ten thousand things which assail us and alienate us from ourselves'. We need to decompress to allow our feelings to surface.

Each and every one of us has qualities, has value. But sometimes we forget that and act against our own happiness and our own interests. Our lists are there to remind us that we are unique, that our lives have meaning, and that everything evolves towards that meaning. The act of writing lists not only allows us to recognise this, it also allows us to write the manifestos of our lives, to see our own potential.

Know exactly who you are. Know your qualities, your good points. Otherwise you will simply be what other people want you to be.

Make a list of these qualities; create your personal manifesto. You can also use this opportunity to write a list of promises to the person you are getting to know: yourself. This will give you the feeling of having accomplished something, and of exercising influence on your life. If you write these promises down in a way that shows gentleness and clarity, and which points to the future in terms of how they can be applied, it will be easy to keep these promises. If you break a difficult problem down into many small steps, it becomes far easier to solve.

It is also very important to write down all your successes. Keeping an account of what you have achieved is a very effective way of reinforcing the power of success and perseverance. A success which you see on the page, written in black and white, is far more persuasive than one confined only to memory. There it may easily be superseded by new memories, memories of little importance, or negative memories. Writing down our successes communicates a clear and strong idea of what we are capable of. It will also allow us to gradually escape the causes of our problems. Success attracts success, as the old adage goes.

Suggested lists:

Things about me which are unique
What I consider to be the value I bring to the world
The moral characteristics which make me stand out
My qualities
Fifty things I am proud of, in ascending order
The subjects I have studied
My talents
What other people like about me
What I can offer to other people
The people who need me
The people whose lives I have brought something to
The people who like me

The reasons these people like me

What I am (try not to use the verb 'to have'. Only list what you are, without mentioning materials goods, qualifications, friends, and so on)

What I could do to simply 'be' (for example, going for a walk in nature, gardening, swimming, watching a sunset, listening to music, kneading dough)

Things I am going to do (write down a deadline, and how you are going to achieve each goal)

Things I will no longer say

Things I will no longer do.

Laughter

Charlie Chaplin said that all you need to succeed in life is a healthy amount of humour and imagination. It is extremely important to laugh. Laughing relaxes you, laughing heals you. To laugh is to be young. Have you ever noticed that the older people get, the less they laugh? And that children will laugh at the smallest thing? Laughter defuses difficult situations and stops us from taking things too seriously. Cancer treatment centres in Kerala hold laughter sessions where the patients and doctors get together simply to laugh. If everyone laughed more, there would probably be fewer stomach ulcers in the world and fewer tragedies. Try not to be too serious, and not to take yourself too seriously. How would you like to live with someone who never laughed?

Suggested lists:

Stories which make me laugh

The films which have made me laugh the most

The situations which have made me laugh the most

The people with whom I laugh most

The types of humour which I respond to most

Ideas for cheering up my friends.

4

Become aware of your thoughts

Our thoughts determine our quality of life

'Energy follows thought.'

Maxim of Eastern medicine

Some people spend their whole lives in a state of indecision and dissatisfaction. This can lead to languor, melancholy or anxiety. These people just don't realise the extent to which negative thinking affects their health and the outcome of their lives. Observe how often you sigh, how often you criticise people, how often you express weakness. These thoughts are like seeds. And if you water them, they will grow in you, and bear poisonous fruit.

In order to become fully conscious of your thoughts, try the following exercise: go to a busy public place and observe your reactions as you watch people. You will notice that you form judgements on everything you see, and that you feel desire, embarrassment, indifference and longing… just by watching strangers!

Now consider the effect these thoughts have on your life in general: what sort of emotions do they provoke? What effect do these emotions have on what you think and what you do? Are these emotions productive or destructive? This exercise (becoming aware of your 'parasitic' thoughts) will help you to eliminate them. It will give you strength.

Most people have no idea of the effect that these silent, secret dialogues have on their lives. But they need to realise that every thought kicks off an emotional chain reaction. And this reaction, while terribly subtle, does affect what we say and do. Negative thoughts change our quality of life for the worse.

Suggested lists (to be written in a café or other public place) on:

The people I am observing (in the left-hand column)

The thoughts and emotions they inspire in me (in the right-hand column)

The thoughts which colour my days.

Banish negative thoughts

In her famous book *You Can Heal Your Life*, Louise Hay – who has first-hand experience of healing after undergoing cancer treatment – writes that by always looking to the positive, and rejecting negative thinking, we can pave the way for a very different outcome. (Although her story is uplifting, I must say there is something potentially harmful about this approach. Not everyone can recover from cancer, and reading things like this may add to the suffering of a terminal patient – not only are they dying, they may also feel guilty for not being able to beat their cancer with positive thinking.)

In any case, she advises that you begin by banning yourself from using phrases which begin 'I must…' and 'I can't…'. These phrases sap our energy. She insists on the fact that words are immensely powerful and that, in certain cases, they can destroy entire nations. But they can also heal. An idea, when repeated many times, becomes reality in people's minds. Thoughts create emotions, which then translate into acts. They are also seeds, and if we tend to them they will take root and bear fruit. How we water them is by giving them energy, and by that she means paying them attention. Attention is a form of energy. Think of all the things which have begun as ideas, then blossomed into plans and finally become a material reality. By feeding your thoughts with energy, they may well translate into a concrete reality.

The list of things we can feel we are victims of is endless – disease, poverty, our boss, our partner; it goes on and on… The main characteristic of a victim is someone who has no choice. But you can 'un-create' the circumstances you have created. Think of your past mistakes as lessons. If you hadn't made mistakes, how could you learn to live better in the future? Everything that happens to us can teach us a lesson.

You can date the entries in your lists. These dates will serve as a point of reference in the future, and will allow you to track the progress of your work on yourself.

Suggested lists:

Positive statements

Five positive things in my mind

Activities which make me think more deeply

The people I know who are happy by nature

Happy things (music, books, films)

Happy places

The smells I like.

Train yourself to stop thinking

Free your psyche, listen to your thoughts, feel the presence of your inner self. No one can ever force us to think something we don't want to think. Our mind is a marvellous tool. It belongs to us and us alone. We are the masters and not the slaves. It is an extraordinary freedom to realise that, with training, we can stop the flow of our thoughts, whenever we want or need to.

Sometimes our thoughts can become monsters. In our normal state, we function on automatic. We have very little control of the workings of our minds, our thoughts and reactions. The majority of people are not masters of their own minds. That is, until they begin to meditate. Meditation allows you to control your mind: to choose your exact thoughts to stop your thoughts and to pick back up a thought process only when you want to.

But how do we control our thoughts, these 'dancing monkeys' as Zen philosophy calls them? The first thing we need to do is observe them and become aware of their presence. But – you say – surely that means we are still thinking? Not exactly. Try to see your thoughts as objects. You are capable of observing and tracking these objects. You can put these objects into your mind at will, and remove them at will. They are like trains coming and going from a station. You have always been told that it isn't possible to control when you stop loving someone, stop desiring someone, stop fearing death. But who decided that? Lists can help here. Pick up a pen and write down, as succinctly as you can, the thought going through your mind at this precise moment. For example, 'I am thinking about thoughts', then,

'Oh, I can hear an aeroplane' 'then' 'What is Y up to right now?'

Look back over what you have written. In the space of a few seconds you have had three discrete thoughts. What now?

Well, naturally you are now trying not to think. Go back to every thought (or entry on your list) and imagine it is a pebble that you have thrown into still water. Wait until the ripples fade before you move on to your next idea. With frequent practice, you will manage to create a moment of nothingness between each thought.

It's just like when you move from one entry on a list to the next. Put your pen down and stop. What is happening in your head? Train yourself to listen to the silence between each thought. If you repeat this exercise as often as you can, you will realise how tiring it is to be constantly thinking. And you will learn that it is possible to stop.

You will succeed – gradually – in making your relationship with things and people less rigid. Everything you do will take on more meaning. List your thoughts – for five or ten minutes at a time – and repeat.

Focus on solutions, not on problems

'Our lives are shaped not as much by our experiences as by our expectations.'

George Bernard Shaw

What we think we believe has very little impact on what we 'viscerally' know. Only the deepest-held convictions have the power to change our reality. Before we undertake something, we need to believe in it. If, in our everyday lives, we create positive images, we have a good chance of creating happiness and success. We can mould our lives with the images and expectations we create for ourselves. Many people want to change but don't know how to go about it. Fix yourself clear, measurable goals. Think in concrete terms. Achieving one goal will encourage you to attack the next. If you only think about your problems, your problems will grow. But if you focus instead on the solutions, everything will improve.

By gaining greater awareness, you will be able to do what you want with your thoughts, with your days and with your life. This power is lying dormant inside you. You can awaken it by making lists. The first step is to reinforce your mental and emotional attitudes.

Suggested lists:

My deepest convictions
My plans for the future
My goals in life.

In choosing your words, you choose the terms of your happiness

'Happiness is being happy, not seeming happy.'

Jules Renard

Every moment of happiness allows you to self-realise, to be yourself. It is important to have such moments in reserve.

We can change who we are by writing down what we choose to see, to feel, to think and to be. Choose what you commit to paper. Extract the things you like from your experience. Do not get weighed down by regrettable things. By rejecting bleak moments and only keeping precious ones, you will create not only your own values but also the person you choose to be. You will feel the delicious power of describing things as you want to describe them. You will create not only your own value system, but also the person you choose to be. A description can never convey reality entirely: it will fashion reality according to how we perceive it. And that is what we should preserve.

By only selecting the most interesting details of your experiences – whether of the books you read, your personal relations or your life aesthetics – you will create your own reality. And, in doing so, you will forge your own perception of the world and become someone who has a rare gift: that of capturing happiness.

We are always struck by thinkers who express the truths we have carried in our subconscious but have been unable to express. Make a list of quotes and phrases which resonate with you. These ideas will then become your own: they will take root in you because they will represent something visceral.

By naming things, we feel as though we possess them a little more, and we derive a tangible satisfaction. Words give us power. And what pleasure could be greater than expressing ourselves in words which exactly describe what we're feeling or, failing that, finding these words in a poem or a piece of prose? These words will become a treasure, a gold mine for us. Many people are frustrated that they cannot express exactly what they feel, but it is an art which can be learnt.

Suggested lists:

Quotes

Poems

Words and phrases which I like.

5

We are our own advocates

How to draw up a list of key questions

*'We do not receive wisdom, we need to go and find it
ourselves, on a journey no one can take for us.'*

Marcel Proust

In his film *Manhattan*, Woody Allen made a list of his reasons to live.
How many times have we done that? Made a list of what we would
like to achieve, accomplish and change.

We are the creators of our own lives. Everything which reinforces
our identity is a positive. Making lists is a way of enriching our existence and allows us to have more agency. What we write is not only
a function of who we already are. It can change who we are, it can
reveal us to ourselves.

Sometimes it is more important to know how to ask and formu-
late questions than to look for answers. These questions can be

drawn from philosophical, spiritual and religious texts, and can become the subject of reflection, introspection and meditation. Théodore Monod wrote that we shouldn't lead our lives as tourists. Everyday life doesn't allow us access to the essence of our existence because everyday life evades the essential. Living without worrying about anything, 'taking it easy', is a form of fleeing. To fulfil your role as a human being, there are questions we inevitably need to face.

Suggested lists:

The different roles I play in life

The person I would like to be, spiritually speaking

What defines me spiritually

My ethical values

The most important things about my past which have led me to the life I live now

The people who have influenced me the most

What I have inherited from my ancestors

The injustices in the world which I feel most strongly about

The qualities of my parents

The things which trouble my conscience most

The principles which I value the most

The freedoms which I think are obvious, and which I take at face value

My reasons for living.

To change things, first visualise them

'In human beings, courage is necessary to make being *and* becoming *possible. An assertion of the self, a commitment, is essential if the self is to have any reality. This is the distinction between human beings and the rest of nature. The acorn becomes an oak by means of automatic growth; no commitment is necessary. The kitten similarly becomes a cat on the basis of instinct. Nature and being are identical in creatures like them. But a man or woman becomes fully human only by his or her choices and his or her commitment to them. People attain worth and dignity by the multitude of decisions they make from day by day.'*

Rollo May, *The Courage to Create*

In order to affect change, it is necessary to visualise your life. This little phrase has changed mine. What could be more fitting, more logical, but also more difficult to achieve?

We think it is useful and important to write 'To Do' lists, or lists of what to bring on holiday. So why not make a list for the longest journey of all – our lives – a list of our ambitions and goals, our convictions and dreams? Why not make a list of directions to follow so that we can reach the summit of our lives? Our future is potentially unlimited. Potentially, we can do whatever we want and go wherever we like. But to do this we need to know what we want and the person we want to be… or become!

You could make a list of small goals to achieve to become closer to that person. The only obstacles are those you create in your own mind.

Make a list of the people, situations and events which you love, and those which you try to avoid. You must know exactly what you want. The more precise, the clearer, the more specific you are in your goals, the more you will resemble the person you aspire to be. Because we transform naturally into the images we create, and these are the images which will stick in our minds. If you bought a thousand-piece jigsaw but didn't have the picture key, what would you do? Perhaps you would manage to complete it in the end, but with great difficulty.

People who know what they want attain their goals far more quickly than others, simply because they know where they are going. And so they know which actions to embark upon and which path to follow.

In the same way that our brains are attracted to images, having precise goals, knowing clearly what we want, acts as a stimulus.

By exploring every day, in our writing, what we can do to move our lives forward, we can make the choices which best reflect our personal views and what we want to achieve on this planet.

Suggested lists:
The books I would like to read
The music I would like to get to know
The works of art I would like to see
The countries I would like to visit
The cultures I would like to discover
The hobbies I would like to master

The things I would like to distance myself from

The place I would like to live in the future

How I see myself in five years' time, in ten years' time, in
    twenty years' time.

6

Make lists to evolve

Sense is first and foremost a direction

'For this gull, the important thing isn't to eat but to fly. One thousands lives, Jon, ten thousand lives! And then one hundred more before we began to understand that something called perfection exists, and then one hundred more to admit that our sole reason for living is to release this perfection, and to claim it...

'What you need to do is continue to discover, on your own and every day, the true Fletcher the Seagull who resides within you. He is the master of you. You must realise this and act accordingly.'

Richard Bach, *Jonathan Livingston Seagull*

Evolution demands transformations. Everything which doesn't evolve diminishes and dies. We must constantly ask ourselves questions to escape from confusion and find the direction in which to take our lives. And to do this, we must call on all the knowledge we have learnt in the course of those lives.

How do we use our senses, intelligence and internal resources to move forward, to nourish ourselves, to guide how we behave around others, to face the fact of death? This is the worry and preoccupation of every human being. These questions are universal and essential because they make us aware of a quest: the quest to give meaning to life. Meaning is first and foremost a direction. And how do we move our plans forward without belief?

Choosing, remembering yourself, revealing the depths of your being… all these things are essential for living a conscious and authentic life.

Embark on self-reflection. Do this for yourself and yourself only. Why do so many people delegate to others the act of thinking for themselves?

The goal of any life should be to create inner harmony. Some philosophers, like Sartre, recognised how fundamental this task was, and called it 'life's project'. This means that all of an individual's actions should be geared towards one goal: giving shape and meaning to your life. And to that end, we must liberate ourselves from the disorder which reigns in our minds, in order to be capable of calling on all the knowledge we have gained in the course of our lives.

Making lists allows us to reflect on, describe and decide on the directions our lives will take. Lists allow us to write ourselves into a story which is bigger than ourselves. A list of questions on life, on the meaning of our lives, on our place in the universe, can guide us in this quest. Meaning is first and foremost a direction. We can be a prisoner to many things: to the present, to our memories, to painful thoughts, to worries about the future. But in order to want to live, we must feel that there is meaning to what we are doing. And so it is necessary to have motivation, to have an ideal future mapped out, to dream and to believe. No one can prove that these things will happen. But nor can the possibility of their happening be denied.

The Japanese know, almost instinctively, because it is written into their culture, that questions about the meaning of life are impossible to answer, and are therefore futile. And so they content themselves with valuing beauty, purity, humility, honesty, work well done, perfection and nature. They have given certain things – the culinary arts, bathing and tea rituals, the manufacture of knives and televisions – a status almost akin to religion. Westerners have always tended to ask themselves questions, to understand the how and why of life. And so they must go down a very long road of reflection before they realise these questions are futile. Sometimes it takes them an entire lifetime to return to the state of being able to live without thinking. 'I think therefore I am' becomes 'I feel therefore I am' or perhaps 'I do not think therefore I am'.

But being means acting according to your conscience. Deep inside ourselves, we always know what is right and what is wrong.

Suggested lists:

How can I evolve?

How can I tangibly live in accordance with my ideas?

What can I do to fight injustice?

What have been my reasons for living up until this point?

What meaning do I want to give my life?

What do I aspire to in life?

Where?

With whom?

What would my life look like if I applied everything I believe in?

My life plans.

What can I bring to the world?

*'I have always thought the actions of men the best
interpreters of their thoughts.'*

John Locke

Imagine for a moment your last day on earth. Make a list of what you have accomplished, the things you are proud of, the things which make you happy. Would your car be on that list? Your television? Your sound system? Your salary? Well, maybe.

But on that list you would perhaps also have written the fundamental elements of a happy life: your friendships, your family, what you have brought to the lives of others, the satisfaction of a life lived honestly. We accumulate possessions and outward markers of status without asking ourselves what success really means. We should beware these false gods – the religions of money, vanity and power – and instead worship at the altar of beauty and of the sacred. We must retain our sense of wonder at the mysteries of the universe.

We can (and should) make a list of all the anomalies in our belief systems. That will lead us to consume differently, to ask ourselves what success is, what a life well lived really looks like.

Why don't we take the time to draw up lists of our beliefs, and therefore try to contribute towards making the world a better place?

Viktor Frankl survived a Nazi concentration camp and went on to become a psychologist and author nicknamed 'the therapist of vitality'. His answer to the question of existence was this: see what you can create (and this can be something artistic, something manual, or simply being a good parent, a good son, a husband or friend). There are thousands of ways of making your contribution to the world. And thousands of ways of being aware that the world can change.

Suggested lists:

How I can live in a more environmentally friendly way

How I can apply my beliefs to my life, concretely

How to put quality ahead of quantity

What I can do to avoid waste

How I use the money I earn

Things my money cannot buy.

Smile at the world and
the world will smile back

*'The sun which shines on us; the stars; the sea; the
clouds in the sky; the sparks of a fire... whether you
live for one hundred years or just a few, you will
never see anything so beautiful.'*

Ménard, poet

The idea of happiness is, in essence, very rich. But it can also lead to mediocrity: it implies that people shouldn't excel themselves and grow beyond the people they already are. It reduces them to the lowest common denominator, to material comfort, instead of elevating them towards greatness. Happiness is neither identifiable nor quantifiable; it belongs to the spiritual world, so to the irrational world.

Isn't our most essential need to be in harmony with ourselves – especially with the most elevated parts of us – and with our environment? We could spend an entire lifetime searching for this sort of ideal – serene and radiant peace – without success, if we lack wisdom and method, and only do what the era we are living in tells us to do. But equally, we can spend our lives watching this serenity unfurl within us.

The Puritans often made lists of their moral transgressions. Benjamin Franklin made a list of the thirteen virtues he had decided to acquire: temperance, frugality, cleanliness, tranquillity, humility, and so on… He even drew a graph of his (slow) progress in every virtue.

But this type of list doesn't bring satisfaction. It is a form of self-censure. Marion Milner, a twentieth-century British diarist, set out to describe all the things she desired and all the things which made her truly happy. Over the course of seven years, she made lists of her desires and the things she took joy in. Step by step, she taught herself how to be happy.

In order to be happy, we must practise. We must remind ourselves how to feel happy. There are many ways to work on this: by rereading your lists, by talking about happiness, weighing up your options wisely, by controlling your desires, by prioritising happiness over money for money's sake, by considering happiness as something to actively engage with, by smiling even when you don't want to, by talking to other people about how to go about finding happiness (instead of complaining about your life). In fact, we owe it to other people to work on these things. In order to love other people, you need to be able to love yourself, and to make yourself happy. Remind yourself of everything you have achieved, of all the moments of happiness which you have experienced. Reread your lists of small pleasures.

The point of these lists isn't to preach, or to reprimand ourselves. The point is to free ourselves from spiritual torpor, to think, to describe, to get closer to reality, to this reality which we lose, little by little, in the course of our lives. And then to decide on the directions we'd like our lives to take. Everyone feels pulsing within them the desire and the need to align themselves with their highest aspirations, even the ones they don't even consciously recognise. To this end, we must realise that we aspire towards absolutes, to a sort of purity which everyday life can only offer us if we live it *consciously*.

Suggested lists:

The happiest people I know

The magical moments in my life

The bravest people I know

The habits and attitudes of older people whom I admire

The things which connect me to who I am on the most
fundamental level

The things which nourish me inwardly

The people I count myself fortunate to have met.

Death

'One thousand plans, ten thousand calculations
A snowflake lands on the fire.'

Thirteenth-century Buddhist poem

The word is taboo in modern Western society. But who doesn't think about death? Can anyone be truly happy without accepting the fact of death as something natural, something that will happen to everyone – to us and everyone close to us? Why does the subject of death frighten us so much? Out of all the 'existential' questions we reflect on, the most common is probably death. The topic only throws up questions because no one has the answer. And so we can write lists of questions…

You can only be truly alive if you have an acute awareness of death. To think about death is to realise the precariousness of life. We need to ask ourselves about life and death because these questions lead to other questions. By reflecting on these questions, we can form our own individual 'ethics'. These will become one of the axes against which we plot the graph of our lives.

Either life has a meaning or life has no meaning. No one knows. But there's nothing preventing us from giving it our own.

By writing lists, we can embark on the path towards finding answers to the questions which we all ask ourselves, or should ask ourselves.

'Death is just a passage towards another form of life, on a different vibratory level,' said Elisabeth Kübler-Ross. This is how we reach the core of ourselves; this is how we keep hold of the thread that attaches us to ourselves. Even if we cannot claim with any certainty that there is life after death, we still have the right to hope for one.

Suggestions of topics to think about:

Is there life after death?

Strange or inexplicable things which people I trust have told me, regarding the existence of life after death

What would I like my legacy to be?

How would I like to spend my last day on earth?

The people I would like to be reincarnated as

What characterises a life well lived?

The plans I've made for my golden old age

The things I would like to do before I die

The best masters, rabbis, priests etc whom I have met or heard of

The things which connect me to the deepest part of myself

Quotes about death.

PART FOUR

1,001 PLEASURES

Imagination
and creativity

We can choose the colours of our lives

'The rain drums on the roof of the van
The animals are curled up asleep
The night, black above the little valleys, is solid; you could
almost cut it into pieces and pile them up
There is no light to be seen
The stream doesn't stop gargling, as though it has a sore
throat. A car goes by on the Mahalt Highway, its lights flash,
here, there, over the van, then it disappears, unreal.'

Emily Carr, chronicles on British Columbia

At the age sixty-one, the American painter Emily Carr decided to move herself, her monkey, her rat and two puppies into a mobile home. She could have feared old age, could have complained about the leaks from her roof, or suffered from self-pity in her solitude. But she chose to live in this unusual way, just as she chose to perceive and describe it in an unusual way. The list-diaries for which she is now known bear testament to this.

We too have the power to paint the tableau of our lives, to choose the colours, the tone and the materials. In doing so, we shape the way in which we perceive the world. By deciding what we want to see, feel, touch, read and do, and then listing these things, we change the way in which we see the world, and therefore how we live. By choosing what we write down, we determine what we do with our lives.

Every day, every minute, can contain multitudes of fascinating things. Writing them down in the form of lists – whether these are made up of single words, phrases or short descriptions – allows us not only to create a reservoir of happiness, but also to develop our senses and sensibilities, along with the creative, imaginative powers we are all born with. This type of list will, in turn, reflect the type of person we choose to be. Creating is one of the greatest joys of being human. It gives us a feeling of transcendence in which we can rise above our egos; it allows us to realise our innate potential.

It's not just painters, photographers, musicians or poets who can create. Every single one of us can, simply with words. We can create ourselves.

Suggested lists:

The charms of each season

The charms of each season of life

Unusual things I'd like to do

Five ways of life I would like to experience

What I like about the place where I live (little noises in the
neighbourhood, the view from my window, and so on).

Escapism and imagination

'In all the miles I have travelled, I cannot say that I have learned what I wanted to learn, because I did not know what I wanted to learn. But I have certainly learned what I didn't know and wanted to know.'

William Least Heat-Moon, traveller and writer

Other peoples' lists inspire and encourage us. They allow us to dream, to open ourselves up, to develop and explore ourselves. This is the best route to self-discovery but also, paradoxically, to forgetting ourselves. We become another person but we also become more ourselves. Life takes on a new dimension. We have access to different personalities.

We must never stop dreaming but, at the same time, we must make the best of the present moment. Only in this way can we realise the thousand joys the future has in store.

Perhaps the best-known list – and one we have all made at some point in our lives – is what we would take to a desert island. When asked this question Marilyn Monroe replied, 'A muscly, tattooed sailor!' I have never heard anyone say, 'The things I already have'.

One of the books which has inspired me to dream the most is the marvellous *Journeys of Simplicity* by the American Quaker author Philip Harnden. It lists the (few) possessions owned by anti-conformist and spiritual figures such as Jesus, Gandhi, pilgrims, missionaries, artists, poets, hermits and explorers (both famous and obscure).

William Least Heat-Moon, an American travel writer, was born in 1939. He went on a tour of America in a van he called Ghost Dancing. Here is what he kept inside:

Sleeping bag and a blanket

Coolman (empty except for a jar of liver pâté a friend gave him
    to make sure he never went hungry)

Rubbermaid basin and a five-litre canteen

Sink

Sears, Roebuck portable toilet

Optimus 8R gas stove (barely bigger than a tin of beans)

Backpack of utensils

Casserole dish

Pan

Marine-issue rucksack of clothes

Toolkit

Notebooks and pencils

Roadmap

Tape recorder

Two Nikon F2 35mm cameras

A list of five objectives

Two guidebooks

Leaves of Grass by Walt Whitman

Black Elk Speaks by John G. Neihardt

Twenty-six one-dollar notes

Four credit cards to buy petrol.

Creativity is in evidence in every aspect of our daily lives: when we prepare a meal, when we arrange flowers in a vase, when we plan a holiday, when we tackle a problem, when we organise our work... In these situations, we are expressing our true nature, our preferences and our originality. When we create, time stops. We think, we express our authentic being. We unlock the secret treasures within us. Our creativity is a deep reservoir – containing infinite possibilities for ideas, for realisations, for discoveries – which fills up through the moments and years of our lives. Creativity laughs in the face of what we can and can't do. It is limitless; a force which can regenerate on its own.

Lists allow us to enter a creative zone. And then it is up to us how much we explore it.

Sit in silence, then begin to write. Throw yourself into it. It doesn't matter if, at the beginning, you don't like what you write. Persist. You will be very surprised by what you are capable of producing. Making lists helps you to develop your imagination, to come out of your shell, to escape the prison of your current thinking. And that in turn allows you to transcend the everyday, to break open the doors which are closed to us. The world around us disappears; we leave it behind by entering the domain of our thoughts and dreams. Surrender yourself to the pleasure of feeling what is coming from your own mind. Creation is play, pure and simple. And who knows, perhaps it will lead to a life project, or to a work of art. Depending on how inspired you are feeling, these lists can even become a form of poetry, if only because you are focusing on what brings you pleasure and devoting your full attention to that.

Suggested lists:

All the places in the world where I would like to build my house

All the lives I would like to lead

The professions I dream of

The country or countries where I would like to live, or at least
    spend a few years in

The person I would like to be

What I would take to a desert island

What I would take in my van for a round-the-world trip.

Small nothings

Read *Schott's Miscellany* as inspiration. It is a unique collection of essential small nothings, a sort of index, where Dante's *Inferno* rubs shoulders with care instructions for linen; caviar with the Celsius scale; the names of golf scores with the spiciness of chillies; facts about John Lennon's cat with *The Twelve Labours of Hercules*. And a thousand other snippets, which are as amusing as they are eclectic.

Reading this wonderful book will immediately make you want to write your own list of 1,001 things which are as amusing as they are eccentric.

Suggested lists:

Names of oolong Chinese teas

The different words for shades of grey

What I would do if I were invisible

Everything relating to rain

Scenes from romantic films which take place in a snowy
New York.

Lists to embellish life:
discover your own aesthetic

'Flowers are beautiful
The moon is beautiful
But, above all, the heart which sees these things is beautiful.'

Zen proverb

We can all make our lives more beautiful. But in order to do that, we need to discover our own aesthetic. Lists give us the opportunity to shape our tastes, informed by a thousand details which we notice in the world, and to immerse ourselves in these. Artists devour images before they come up with their own. Go for a drive or a bike ride, a walk or a train journey. Observe different landscapes and qualities of light, whether you're looking out of a car window, in an alleyway, at the seaside or on the top of a mountain. All these things will act as a catalyst to creative thought. What a pleasure it is to drive or walk in the rain, to explore the back roads or the architectural details of your town, to get off the beaten path. If you don't have a car, take a bus, a boat, a bike or simply walk. Allow yourself to become submerged in the tide of images, devour the world with your eyes. Think of all the variety life contains. Let what you are seeing fill you up. List everything you notice in a café: the people, their conversations, the smells, the noises, the colours, the decor... observe life as it is happening around you. Become a silent spectator; open your eyes and prick up your ears.

What makes life beautiful? Search, dig deep, pay close attention to yourself and to others, to what you read in books, anywhere, in fact. This way, you can refurbish your head and redecorate your life. Isn't that an exalting pastime? Making lists helps you to live more fully. Reality is created day after day, in small increments. There is a lot to be said for a life lived day to day. Our lives are like symphonies. Make a list of the things you like in a certain place (for example, a hotel, a friend's house… then it will be easier to incorporate these things into your own life), and of your favourite things (for example, a film, a certain decor, a salad). What you need is concrete detail. If you like a biscuit, write down the brand and the shop which sells it. Write down the names of streets which evoke memories in you, write down foreign names if you've actually met a person who has that name. Anything can adorn your life, if you simply apply yourself.

Suggested lists:

The words or expressions which I find pleasing

My favourite cafés, parks, temples, films, flowers, architects, types of incense, perfumes, noises, types of bubble bath

The most beautiful rivers, mountains and forests which I have seen

The most beautiful natural spectacles I have seen (for example, sunsets, the Northern Lights)

My favourite haikus

Descriptions of people in the street who have caught my eye.

Elegant things

'Elegant things:
A rosary in rock crystal
Snow on wisteria and plum trees.'

The Pillow Book by Sei Shonagon

Elegance belongs to the realm of perfectionism. There is always scope to improve upon elegance; to push the boundaries of purity and beauty. Strive for beauty in every domain or your life: in the objects you own, the places you live in, indeed the body you live in. Beautiful things unite a person with the world around them, creating harmony between man and the universe. Seek out beauty for the emotions it incites, for the pleasure it brings. Beauty cannot be bought. Beauty is harmony, especially with the most noble part of ourselves. Beauty is having a calm heart.

Special moments

'A fire made of twigs
Happy moments
Tête-à-tête.'

Kobyashi Issa

Every moment contains a small piece of eternity. The quality of a moment depends on the attention you pay it. And for that to happen, you have to get into the mindset of dreaming. Our capacity for pleasure, ecstasy, perfection, for refined emotion – for luxury, essentially – is learnt and built. Aristotle once said, 'The more we develop our capacity for contemplation, the more we develop our capacity for happiness'.

There is a time for everything, an activity for every moment. The sense of not having enough time is a common one. But this comes only from lacking the discipline to accord yourself room for pleasure. Dissatisfaction and frustration derive from a mixture – or rather a confusion – of different things. We work too much but we don't work effectively. And when we want to switch off, we don't switch off entirely. Why not take a moment to write a list of what you would do on a perfect day, with your tasks broken up by moments of true rest, of your personal rituals? Give yourself an extra fifteen minutes in the morning to have breakfast in a café before you go to work, to buy flowers on a Thursday, do the shopping on a Saturday morning, have one routine for work and one for your small pleas-ures... You can also write down the emotions you will feel on that day, or rather the aspects which please you.

Make the most of every day. Think of tasks you previously thought of as chores as pleasures. Walking the dog can be a pleasure, as can buying groceries. Even a day when nothing in particular happens can be fully appreciated. Every day, take the time to contemplate the simple pleasures of life. Every day well lived becomes a happy yesterday.

Suggested lists:

An ideal day

The pleasures which become a loop in time (a free weekend, an afternoon of shopping, an evening out, half an hour of meditation, a sabbatical year)

The small pleasures which break the monotony of everyday life

My diary of outings (cinema, seeing friends)

Writing about my travels

Writing about my holidays.

The pleasures of reading

Since we have come to pleasures of the intellectual variety, here is an extract from the list 'The Pleasures of Reading', published in *Le Monde* on 24 February 2004.

Read a book in bed. Press your right leg against your lover's left. Your lover is also reading a book.

Read your lover's body with your fingertips.

Read or reread French classics when you're on the loo.

If you're worrying about the fate of the heroine, turn to the last lines of your novel to check whether she's still alive.

Read *The Pillow Book* for the umpteenth time. But this time don't read a library copy. Read the copy you've just gone out and bought yourself.

Read while smoking Dunhills.

Begin a book when the train is pulling out of the station; finish it just before you arrive.

Reread your favourite book.

Realise, realise with wonder, that you can read a book back to front.

Read quotes which deserve to be savoured. Write them in a notebook. Conserve them like treasures.

Read the last page of a book so you know the end of the story.

Watch someone read a book you love.

Pause before you turn the final page.

Love a book beloved by someone you love.

Look at a pile of books.

Put aside books to read tomorrow, next week, next month… to read later.

At the library, look at the person next to you out of the corner of your eye (while reading Schopenhauer).

Read to someone.

Read a poetry book in a voice which is neither loud nor soft.

Put off the pleasure of reading a book you really want to read.

Stop reading and look at the sky.

Read all night long.

Why not write down in a notebook the books you have read, with the place where you read them and the date when you finished them? This list will act as a marker in time. Here is an extract from mine:

1995, Paris, *The Great Gatsby* by F. Scott Fitzgerald.

1998, Lisbon, *I Am A Cat* by Soseki Natsume.

1987, *Poems* by Emily Dickinson, under the teaching of Francis Berces, my favourite university professor.

1985, *Wisdom of Insecurity* by Alan Watts, on fresh summer evenings in Sam's living room in Aptos, California, while sipping home-made cocktails by a wood fire.

1989, *The Book of Tea* by Kakuzo Okakura, in my small room in Tokyo which had six *tatami* on the floor.

1987, *Gateway to Wisdom* by John Blofeld, on an internal flight in Thailand.

1987, *Walden* by Henry David Thoreau, in Banff National Park in Canada, while camping with Sandy, Mark and Jeff. A dream holiday during our carefree student days.

1990, *Zen and the Art of Motorcycle Maintenance* by Robert Pirsig, during a New Year holiday when it snowed in Tokyo.

1994, *Gift from the Sea* by Anne Morrow Lindbergh, in a rented studio near Central Park, New York.

1996, *Zen, Sitting Simply: A Zen Monk's Commentary on the Fukanzazengi* by Master Dogan, in a temple in Nagoya, when everyone else was asleep.

1997, *Notes from my monk's cabin* by Kamo no Chomei. I read it in Tokyo but I'd borrowed the book from a library in Harajuku.

1999, *The Private Papers of Henry Ryecroft* by George Gissing, given to me by Hajime in Tokyo.

2003, *Reflections in a Golden Eye* by Carson McCullers, when I was staying with Jean and Yukio, while watching the squirrels on the lawn.

2004, *Crazy Clouds* by Rikku. My mother gave it to me.

2004, *The Hermeneutics of the Subject* by Foucault, given to me in a bookshop near to Aligre market.

2004, *The Importance of Living* by Lin Yutang, recommended by Claude B., in Paris.

2005, *Journeys of Simplicity: Travelling Light* by Philip Harnden. I read it in Tokyo then gave it to John in Paris.

2006, *Le vrai classique du vide parfait* by Lie Tseu, which I read on the Eurostar.

2007, *The Dawn of Day* by Nietzsche, given to me by Hajime in Paris.

2007, *Ivresses de brume et de brouillard*, a collection of Buddhist poetry written by Korean monks. I read it one morning, in candlelight, as classical music played in the *Gamin de Paris*, in the Marais.

By making a record of what you read, you will feel as though you are holding onto moments of happiness. Reading can give us wonderful memories. Write notes on what you read. Every book we have read has changed us, and made us the person we are today. Reading is a journey, an adventure and a meeting of minds. Making notes on what you read is like making stopovers: revising what you have felt and thought, and putting this into your own words. Reading and making notes are inextricably linked: one feeds the other and vice versa. If books have really influenced us, we can always reread them. As Cioran said, the most important books aren't the ones we read. They're the ones we reread.

Suggested lists:

The books I have read

My literary references

Books on my 'to read' pile

Books on my 'to reread' pile

Notes on the books you have read.

Culture

The same applies to other art forms. Make a list of the films, exhibitions and plays you have seen. This not only helps you to remember the names of the artists, the works and your personal responses, but also to hold onto moments of pleasure. Programmes, tickets and other printed material will only clutter up your cupboards. They will not bring the same pleasure as seeing, on your very own list, what you personally gained from the experience.

Suggested lists:

Films I have watched (a friend of mine makes clippings from
L'Officiel des Spectacles, sticking the entries for films she
has seen into her ring-bound notebook)

Exhibitions

Conferences

Museums

Places of architectural interest

Ballets

Concerts

Plays.

Lists in the form of haikus

'In the moonlight, I go home and sit down to write a letter.'
'Dying embers, I cannot waste them, I fan them gently.'
'A small country newspaper, I read it in a minute.'

Three haikus by Hosai Ozaki

These haikus, written on only one line (so not in their traditional form) read almost like simple phrases. But what intensity they have, what concision, what poetry.

You too can derive inspiration from the haiku, and write down, in lists of phrases, the experiences which you want to turn into memories. Everything in life is a source of poetry. Haikus are juxtapositions, they're associations of ideas, they're collages of words. They are details, accumulating. Make your own collection of phrases and dive in. If you practise, you will learn to express an awful lot in very few words.

AN EXCERPT FROM MY 'JAPANESE SKETCHES'

The tobacco seller in Ayoamo: his face like a sheaf of silk paper
The distinguished skeleton of a professor of calligraphy
The funeral of K.Y.: the kimonos were severe and sumptuous
An old Ryokan in Nagano. There is a fire. A bitter tea brews on three torches
Small gardens in old Tokyo: there is not a single leaf on the ground

Arai Ryokan, stones, moss, wood, the gloss on the mats
Wakayama, the countryside grey, brown and green
A fish wrapped up like a jewel: a present from one of my
    students
A paddy field; a heron amidst the reeds; a Ming vase?

Recipes for happiness

'And now with some pleasure I find that it's seven; and must cook dinner. Haddock and sausage meat. I think it is true that one gains a certain hold on sausage and haddock by writing them down.'

Virginia Woolf

How do you find true happiness in life? Is there a point to life? Or are these questions pointless and unanswerable? The Chinese would say these questions are more practical than philosophical. Their response is simple: take pleasure in life. It is natural to take pleasure from life, and for that reason you cannot separate the material and spiritual dimensions of pleasure. There is a material side to a picnic, for example, and a spiritual side to a picnic.

Writing a list of our favourite moments can sum up what we mean by a 'happy' life. These scraps of happiness, when viewed as a whole, will prove to us that true happiness is not derived from showing a certain version of ourselves to other people, or from trying to project what they want to see. They will show us that true happiness comes from taking pleasure in thousands of small, unexpected, everyday things: the sound of a faraway piano, a burst of laughter, a smile, the flight of migrating birds, a beautiful dream. Such things remind you that even in difficult times, every moment contains something good. Making a list of these things can change your life.

Happiness is less a function of external events than the way in which we experience them. And how we experience them depends in turn on our ability to feel and perceive, with every sense, each new experience. It depends on our capacity to marvel at these experiences, and to appreciate life and the changes it brings.

Diaries are often a receptacle for negative emotions. But making lists of good and beautiful things lends a positive power to what we write, and brings us positivity.

If we commit happy things and happy moments to paper, our future self will remember how to be happy. Think of these lists as recipes. Recipes for happiness.

SMALL PLEASURES

Listening to Bach while watching the rain

Watching black and white films late at night when everyone else is asleep

Wrapping myself in a good, warm coat and going for a winter walk

Going on a picnic

Listening to frogs croaking on a summer night

Being on the deck of a boat in open seas

Looking over Paris from a rooftop, or from the Eiffel Tower

Taking a funicular

The moment when an aeroplane cuts through the clouds

Watching champagne bubbles strike the crystal then rise to the surface in an elegant ballet

Walking barefoot on a thick carpet

Taking a London cab

Rising before daybreak, knowing I can take a nap

Cutting the stalks of a big bunch of lilies, still damp with rose
water

Waking up to the smell of coffee and warm bread

Folding fresh laundry

Going to sleep in a room where incense has been burning

Wooden floors which creak under your feet

Going to a thermal spring when it's snowing outside

Polished things: leather, furniture

Candles in the semi-darkness of a room

Letting your hair dry in the sun.

Suggested lists of small pleasures:

By season

In the course of the day

By country

Shared with someone I love

Enjoyed alone

In certain places.

2

The pleasures of the senses

Do we really get the most out of our senses?

Before thought, there is sensation. Everything comes to us via our senses. To recognise their existence, to refine them, to heighten them, is to enjoy a fuller life.

What can you hear now, right now? What can you smell? Are you sitting comfortably?

If we do not put our senses to good use, they become less sharp. And that, in turn, stops us from being fully able to appreciate the joys of life. Do we know how to savour daytime smells and night-time smells, winter smells and summer smells?

Beauty embellishes the ordinary and it demands our attention: we need to cultivate our sense of beauty. And that is why it is important to take the concrete step of naming our sensations precisely. Precision breeds quality.

Our body is the filter through which we apprehend the world. In order to better appreciate the world, we need to work meticulously on all our senses. We need to study what we are seeing, hearing, smelling, tasting and touching.

To lose one sense is to be deprived of one part of our body. It is possible to maintain, protect and develop our sensory faculties at any age – the only prerequisite is wanting to. Recognising different types of wine, tasting them, relishing them, having the words to describe them, defining the bouquet, the flavour... all these things can be learnt. Afterwards, we will be surprised at how little we perceived before, how much pleasure had escaped us. Every sommelier, in the course of their training, will write down a list of the wines they have tasted, with tasting notes on each.

To live fully, we must recognise the reality of our senses, then actively try to refine them, correct them, sometimes deny them, in order to bring new flavours to our lives. The more we work on our senses, the more joy, memories and delight they will bring us. Our senses have the power to transport us into a world of marvels. And lists can open the door to that world...

Sight

'Things which can be improved by being painted:

A pine tree

Autumnal countryside

A mountain village

A winter landscape, in extreme cold.'

Sei Shonagon, *The Pillow Book*

All of us, when we look at things, have images in our heads. And looking is a skill which can be learnt. A photographer will immediately recognise a photogenic face; an aesthete the beauty of the light on a summer's evening; a chef the most delicate fish. To seize the nuances of a colour, and to make them real to you, you need words. Otherwise these things remain invisible to us. Three centuries ago in Japan, manufacturers of dye for kimonos had names for 110 shades of black and 90 shades of grey. The Inuit use around fifteen different adjectives to describe the colour of snow.

Every one of us could, potentially, differentiate between thousands of colours. But in order to do so, we would need the terms to describe them. Learning new distinctions broadens the palette of our knowledge. We must build our vocabulary of colours. The same process applies to shapes, to the quality of light and the quality of shadows.

THE THINGS I LIKE TO LOOK AT

Shooting stars

Swifts dancing in the summer sky

Paris, from a rooftop

A spider catching a mosquito in its web

Poppies

Shadows in a candlelit room

Falling snow

The infinite variety of human faces.

Over to you...

Suggested lists:

Expressions relating to the visual realm

What I like to look at

Colours

Shadows, iridescent things, gradations, reflections

Clouds

Two-dimensional shapes

Three-dimensional shapes

Surfaces

Lines

Silhouettes

Blurred and faded things.

Smell

'When nothing is left of a long gone past, when the people are
dead and the objects long since destroyed, the only things
which will remain are smell and taste, more precarious yet
more alive, more immaterial, more persistent, more true, yes
they will remain, like souls, remembering, waiting, hoping,
when all else lies ruined, and they will, these impalpable
droplets, prop up the edifice of memory, without faltering.'

Marcel Proust, *Swann's Way*

Perhaps even more so than images, tastes or sounds, smells possess a rare power to instantly evoke memories. They can take us far away, or far back in time; they can bring us right back to a scene from childhood, to a person, a place or a situation. Whether used to seduce, or simply to give us pleasure, they bring charm to our lives. They allow us to project a specific image; they add something subtle but indispensable to how we are perceived. Smells distinguish us, they give us confidence, they reveal us to ourselves.

They have therapeutic uses, too. They have the power to calm us, to change our mood, to fight stress and anguish. The popularity of aromatherapy proves this. Coma patients have been known to cry tears of joy in the presence of certain scents (see *La saveur du monde*, by David Le Breton). Breathing in certain scents can restore the will to live in people who have lost it, evoking feelings which have been profoundly buried and repressed. In sixteenth-century Europe, soldiers used pungent spices to help the wounded forget their pain. Today, some doctors use essential oils to help patients relax when they are coming round after surgery (for example, when they are anxious, waiting for the results of biopsies). To develop and attune your sense of smell is not only a pleasure, it can be a key to unlocking happiness.

THE THINGS I LIKE TO SMELL

Cedar and pine in sawmills
The dust in Grand Central Station in New York
The fur of Shushu the cat
A match which has just been struck
Waxed wood
The ink I use to write my morning journal
A kitchen where bread is being baked
Skin

Over to you…

Suggested lists:
Smells specific to certain places and things
My olfactory pleasures
The smells of my childhood
My favourite smells in nature
The words and expressions relating to smells which I like (e.g. teas, lichens, inks).

Taste

'Peeling a pear
Tender drops of moisture
Glistening on the knife.'

Haiku by Shiki Masaoka (1867 – 1902)

The art of tasting, of savouring, is also something which can be learnt. Without this education, our sense of taste will not reach its full potential. We will not achieve the greatest possible quality of life, of health, of sensibility, of awakened consciousness.

We can only appreciate taste by slowly chewing every mouthful. Train yourself with a grape, an almond or a grain of brown rice. Focus on that single mouthful. Before you swallow, smell, taste, chew, really work your jaw. Only swallow when you are sure you have experienced everything you possibly can. As you chew, you will discover different tastes. Try to describe these different tastes in the most exact terms you can find. What taste does a beetroot have, a sprig of coriander, a mocha?

The more vocabulary you have for what you are tasting, the more awareness you will have of sensations which up to this point have eluded you. And the more nuance you will bring to what you experience. By learning that champagne tastes of raspberries, you will be able to fully appreciate its smells and flavours. You will be surprised by how much you have been oblivious to.

Describing your sensations is a way of broadening your intellect and stoking your curiosity. It will also give you more joie de vivre.

Your universe will expand, you will find more opportunities to experience pleasure and raise your consciousness. Every new pleasure turns into a new experience.

THE THINGS I LIKE TO TASTE:

Salmon roe, which burst under my tongue
The bitter aftertaste of Tungting tea
A cucumber from the garden
Chutney, and the sensation of it on my tongue
The freshness of a lettuce leaf, in the same mouthful as some
    cheddar
Sea urchin sushi.

Over to you...

Suggested lists:
Words and phrases relating to food and drink
The names of foods, drinks and dishes which I am discovering
    for the first time
The tastes I like
The tastes I don't like
Foodstuffs classified under five categories: salty, sweet, acidic,
    bitter, sour.

Touch

'Happiness is also touch. Thomas walked barefoot
from the smooth floor to the cold stone in the corridor
and on the doorstep, then to the round pebbles
glistening with drying dew.'

Czetaw Mitosz, *The Issa Valley*

Albert Palma, author of *Geido, The Way of the Arts*, says in an interview with writer Philippe Nassif: 'The senses, once awakened, transfigure reason.'

Touching, reaching out, approaching, stirring, perceiving, feeling, getting to know... These acts happen every day. We have no choice but to be in contact with the world which surrounds us. And we can only gain awareness of ourselves by touching and feeling, in every sense of those terms.

Touch allows us not only to communicate but also to evaluate, to appreciate, to express our emotions and pleasures, to express the simple fact of being alive (a patch of skin the size of a pound coin contains millions of cells). Feeling and touching are therefore essential parts of self-awareness. If a man lost his sense of touch, Rodin said to Camille Claudel, he would die. According to the type of touch we receive, we can become calmer, more excited or more conscious of the world around us.

THE THINGS I LIKE TO FEEL

The heat of the sun through windows in winter

The first flakes of snow landing on my face

The hands of a masseur

The first crisp evenings after a heatwave

A leather jacket

A raspberry jam pip cracking under my tooth.

Over to you…

Suggested lists:

What touch means to me

What feeling means to me

The ways in which I can touch other people

Textures which give me tactile pleasure

Textures which irritate me

The feelings of touch which are essential to me.

Hearing

'I hear the sounds of the Heywood stream, pouring into Fair
Heaven lake. This sound brings an inexpressible comfort
to my senses. It really feels as though the water is coursing
through my bones. I listen to it with an unquenchable thirst.
It calms my fever. It changes my circulation: I believe it is in
synchronicity with the blood which runs through my veins.
What am I listening to, if not the pure cascades within me,
the currents which run into my heart?'

Henry David Thoreau, *Walden*

One of the things most dangerous to our health is noise pollution. All day long we are assailed by sounds, by noise, by music. It would be impossible to list all the things we hear, but we can look out for them, as much to protect and defend ourselves from sounds as to enjoy the ones we take pleasure in. And, with this goal in mind, making a list of sounds can enable us to be more sensitive to our environment, and can give us the means to improve our environment (in so far as we can). A thousand different forms of aural violence insinuate their way into our days, against our will. Why do governments not launch campaigns against noise pollution, in the same way they have against smoking?

THE THINGS I LIKE TO HEAR

Footsteps in the snow

Waves

The tweet-twoo of an owl

Rain on canvas (in a tent or on an umbrella)

Walking on a carpet of leaves which crunch underfoot

The crackle of burning wood

Foghorns on the Thames.

Over to you...

Suggested lists:

The sounds which I can change, reduce in volume, or suppress
    entirely (my ringtone, the Velcro on my sports bag, the
    sound of my chair scraping on the tiles)

What I like listening to

The noises in my immediate environment (this is something to
    pay attention to when moving house)

The sounds which I like in a certain place

Things I listen to when I'm in a particular mood.

Nourish yourself with music

'If music be the food of love, play on.'

William Shakespeare

If I place a lot of importance on music in this chapter, it is because it is one of the most important conduits for feeling and emotion. Some people insist that music can bring just as much pleasure as love or food. Sometimes, music can replace words. Playing Mahler while watching the sunset, or Bach's *Siciliana* at a funeral, can express so much more than words ever could.

Music can seem like a superficial pleasure. But this is not the case: it can incite feelings so powerful they can order or reorder our lives. Confucius went as far as to think it could be a civilising force. It can help us to restructure our minds, to chase away boredom and anxiety, to reassure us, calm us, to stimulate us... And if it can orchestrate our emotions, then we can take control of how it does that.

The emotions which music evokes in us are far too intense to be taken lightly. For me, listening to Chopin when I'm feeling low, or rock music when I'm on edge, is like pouring so much cream into my coffee that I feel sick, or drinking a double espresso just before I go to bed.

Music is a vital art form. The pleasure it gives is carnal. Its vibrations enter the body, caress it, make it tremble. By partaking of the pleasure of listening to music – an act which may seem absurd but is essential and marvellous – we can get to the heart of reality. And by that I mean the heart of the following paradox: that it is only when we transcend meaning that can we find the most profound meaning in the world.

Choosing what we feed our minds is just as important as choosing what we feed our bodies. Technology allows us to make playlists which correspond exactly to our mood, to where we are, to our circumstances. You can attach a mood and a colour to a song, pack songs away for winter so they will always belong to spring, keep some songs for morning, some to fight sadness, some to indulge this very sadness. These are the choices true music lovers make, and it is possible to learn how to be one. Why not listen to bossa nova while looking at snow-topped mountains, someone once said to me? It is up to us to create the musical connections we need to furnish each moment. It is very rare to find albums which we can listen to on a loop and still take pleasure from. Why wait for a Bach fugue to finish before switching to the next prelude, if that's what you really want to listen to?

THE THINGS I LIKE TO LISTEN TO

The sounds of nature

Classical music, while cooking

The Beatles, periodically

Vivaldi, when I need to recharge my batteries

Certain film scores (*The English Patient*, *The Way We Were*,
   The Scent of Green Papaya) – I could listen to them for ever
   when I'm reading or writing

Songs from my childhood, back when I lived with my parents

Ancient Korean instrumental music, when I don't want to feel
   a single thing

Songs which remind me of happy times (I have a song for each of my former lovers)

Japanese music – *koto* or *shakuachi* – when I need to recentre myself

The songs of 'my generation' or my 'youth' (Simon and Garfunkel, Bob Dylan, David Bowie…)

Post-war American jazz, especially in the evenings when everything is calm.

Over to you…

Suggested playlists, genre by genre, for:

Relaxing

Working

Writing

Reading

Listening to alone

Getting to sleep

Dinner parties

Housework

Bath time

Getting out of bed

Yoga

Meditation

Listening to the rain

Romantic nights in

Nostalgic moments

Remembering certain holidays, certain people.

Combinations of senses

In order to understand your senses better, it is necessary to work on them in isolation. But it is only by combining them that we can access life's true stimulations. Chinese tea served in a heavy, coarse pot will not bring you the same pleasure as the same tea served in a delicate Chinese teapot, and drunk from appropriate cups. Eating asparagus in winter doesn't bring the same pleasure as eating the first fresh asparagus of spring, rediscovered after almost a year, like lilies or grilled chestnuts. Watching a wood fire burn brings pleasure to all the senses…

FUN LISTS: TRIOS OF PLEASURE

In order to maximise your small pleasures, come up with lists of three things which go together. For example:

Massage, incense, gentle music
Coffee, mint chocolates, a cigarette
An armchair, a lamp, a pile of old books
Goat's cheese, brown bread and a little brandy for a picnic in
the mountains.

The pleasure of rereading yourself

Our lists describe our dreams, aspirations, reflections, personal experiences, the pleasures we have enjoyed or have in store, our favourite quotations and poems... They can become the most precious collection we have in our lives. But whatever the subject of our lists, the most important thing is always to keep them. Our lists bring us pleasure, and shed new light on who we are. We will only experience the true pleasure of rereading when we have forgotten what our lists contain. Then we can savour our memories as we would a vintage wine. The older the list, the higher its value.

And what a pleasure it is to reread the lists yourself, to turn the pages of the atlas of your life, to see before your eyes everything you have loved, everything that has moved you, the richness of the universes which belong only to us.

PART FIVE

LISTS: A USER'S MANUAL

1

Lists and their support

Your notebook is
your closest companion

'The moleskin, the iconic little black notebook used by Van Gogh, Matisse and Hemingway, and on which I write down colours and faces, anecdotes, things I have seen, titles of songs, names of hotels, quotes I've magpied, by anyone from Yourcenar to Picabia, Aristotle to Bob Dylan... It is a small treasure trove, to which I have added much over the years: Navajo and Kurdish proverbs, statistics, slang overheard on the street or in a bistro, trivialities I read in magazines, thoughts which cross my mind during journeys, assignments and interviews which become the source material for a book or an article... I often find the titles of my books and films, or the inspiration for a key phrase in a speech, in my notebook. These little black books really are priceless. They are my main tool.'

Fall Down Seven Times, Get Up Eight by Philippe Labro

The notebook is where we collect our mental images, doodles, personal writing, passages we have copied, dreams and travelogues. It is our closest companion. Many people feel the need to make lists, to take notes, to collect ideas, images and thoughts. By sorting them, and recording them in a systematic way, over the course of time and the course of our thoughts, we can connect different parts of our lives and develop certain subjects.

Sometimes the best ideas strike us when we are least expecting it, like flashes of lightning. And they disappear just as quickly. So we feel frustrated that we have not retained these ideas. We have to be realistic: we cannot retain everything. We also have to be disciplined in writing things down: at any one moment, so many ideas are crossing our minds. The notebook is our companion when we wander and when we need consolation; it allows us to set down our thoughts at any time. The notebook is an indispensable back-up for our personality. For some people it becomes an obsession. Always carry one with you.

The notebook as a fetish object

One day, in Tokyo, I was lucky enough to visit an exhibition of old notebooks and I was particularly impressed by an eighteenth-century Filofax (Filofax has of course become one of the best-known brands today).

The concept was invented by an American farmer who wanted to keep a 'file of facts' in a systematic and rational way. She wrote down everything from her everyday life, work life and personal life: harvests, receipts, lists of seeds to buy for the next season, new recipes, the neighbours who came to visit. And you could see from the neatness of her slanted handwriting, and the long, perfectly aligned columns of figures, how organised and honest this woman must have been.

I will also never forget the tiny red notebooks which contained Nabokov's notes – displayed next to his black, thick-framed glasses with smoked-glass lenses, and his enormous, now tarnished Montblanc pen – in the window of the entrance hall to the New York Public Library.

A good notebook will become an extension of yourself, a part of yourself, and without it you will feel empty.

Like handbags, notebooks can become obsessions. Some people are obsessed by leather-bound notebooks. Staying true to a good old notebook, despite its stains and worn corners, can be a source of pleasure. Here are some of the particular pleasures you can derive from your notebook: seeing it fill up; seeing it become worn; feeling its blank pages against your fingertips, soft and smooth, fine and supple, or brittle with age; looking at the colour of your words change from red or blue or green (for your dreams) or gold (when you are writing or copying a poem) to black as time goes by; smelling the pages and the ink; maintaining the same presentation when you write, as a ritual, the same paper, the same pen, the same ink; appreciating the refinement of your handwriting; then closing the 'book of your life', hearing the dull thud of its thickness, the click of the lock... These tactile pleasures will go hand in hand with the physical pleasure of writing.

Write the entries in your notebook with the precision you would apply to writing a haiku. Write them in your notebook first so you can avoid mistakes when you copy them into your definitive lists. To this end, you can also write in pencil. Take care with the presentation of your lists: write in neat columns, date your entries. This way, you will be more inclined to persevere in your 'collection'. A badly kept notebook will end up in the bin.

Always use the same notebook. Divide your notebook into sections for different colours of ink and different themes. If you change your system of notation in the course of your notebook, it will not feel the same.

Choosing how to support your lists

The first thing to do when you start making lists is to decide, once and for all, where you are ultimately going to keep them – in a notebook, on a computer or on a memory card? Everyone must make this choice themselves; the key thing is that the space available should be potentially unlimited. Anecdotes, quotes, things which make us laugh, tabloid scandals (and why not)… it doesn't matter what you are collecting in your lists, all that matters is that you are not confined in terms of space, and that you don't scatter entries relating to the same theme across different notebooks. Otherwise, lists stop being lists and lose their raison d'être (to give you an overarching perspective; to allow comparisons to emerge; to give you reference points).

Notebooks containing many different sections – for example, for addresses and email addresses – weigh us down so much that we end up simply leaving them at home and going back to writing things down on scraps of paper or on Post-it notes, which we then stuff in our pockets or in our bag, or between the pages of a book. Or we try to keep everything in our heads. We lose our way. We end up writing things on calendars or notes left on the breakfast table, or in the bottom of a bag. We end up constantly looking for the thing we have lost at the very moment when we need it. We live in fear of losing the precious slip of paper where we've written the number we urgently require. What we need in life is a good system of organisation, one we can trust. Something practical, which we can always have to hand. Everything should be written down on paper. But never begin your lists in notebooks, no matter how thick they may be: the point of a list is to allow flexibility, to allow you to regroup different elements or add to them. Once your notebook is full, you can't add anything.

NOTEBOOKS AND ORGANISERS

By its very definition, a list can be extended at will, and once the notebook has been filled it must be replaced. My suggestion is to have two support systems. First, in the notes section of your pocket organiser, write down ideas as and when they come to you, even when you're on the go. Secondly, at home, use your computer as a big ring binder. This way, you can regularly go through the scribbles in your pocket organiser and transfer what you want to keep into your main lists, which you keep perfectly classified and ordered. If your ring binder or organiser really is full, it is possible to buy special organisers in which to archive all your old lists.

'Bible'-size organisers (so just bigger than a paperback) with 30mm ring binds will give you the most capacity while fitting easily into a day bag. On the first pages, you can write an index of the lists the book will contain so you can locate them easily. Order them alphabetically and not numerically. The letter A can cover many different topics, just like in a dictionary. This system is simple, practical and very logical indeed.

Broad categories:

1. Daily life
2. Health, diet, hygiene
3. Social life
4. Personal life
5. Miscellaneous.

Subcategories: daily life

1. Shopping lists
2. Clothes
3. Finances
4. 'To Do' list
5. Housekeeping tricks
6. Gardening
7. ... and so on.

Subcategories: health, diet, hygiene

1. Recipes
2. Medicines to take in case of X or Y illness
3. Health notebook
4. Diet notebook
5. ... and so on.

Subcategories: social life

1. Invitations
2. Presents given and received
3. Meetings with friends
4. Cards received
5. Cards sent.

Subcategories: personal life

1. My dreams
2. My problems and possible solutions
3. My 1,001 little pleasures
4. What I read
5. ... and so on.

Subcategories: miscellaneous (to be sorted by precise topic, for example)

1. Travel
2. Visits to botanical gardens (for example, if parks are your passion)
3. The cycles of the moon
4. Combat sports
5. ... and so on.

This system of classification is just one example. Only with time will you find the system which suits *you* best; two people's systems will never be the same. Making lists forces you to get to know yourself, to find yourself.

If you spend a lot of time in front of a computer, you can of course make your lists on a computer. Here, for example, is the system one of my friends uses. She is a very busy journalist who flits all over the world, and yet she is perfectly organised and calm. Her list is structured around broad categories of activities, all of which have implications in different spheres.

Media, written press, communication:

- Journalists
- Commissions
- Documentaries made
- Articles written
- Radio
- ... and so on.

Dossiers of press clippings, kept in big binders:

- Terrorism
- Relationships
- Women
- Babies
- ... and so on.

Personal notes:

- Finances
- Astrology
- Her artwork
- ... and so on.

Dossier on 'M' (her husband):

- Emails
- Jokes
- Our happiest moments
- Our marriage
- Photos of us.

Finances:
- Invoices outstanding
- Expenses to claim
- Reminders
- ... and so on

Passwords:
- PIN codes and banking passwords
- Passwords for websites
- Flat codes.

Dossiers per country:
- Things to do
- People to see
- Activities
- Why I like the country.

Work in progress:
- Articles to write
- Research to do
- People to contact.

ON PAPER

Your paper should be as thinly lined as possible so you can maximise how much you write on each page. Thinly lined paper demands clear, precise writing. People with big handwriting should obviously buy a bigger notebook. And if you are writing a lot of lists, why not put them in separate notebooks? For example, one for Everyday Life, one for My Self-Portrait, and so on.

ON A COMPUTER

In French, a computer is called an 'ordinateur' – the derivation comes from the word 'to order'. Your computer will even offer you templates for lists. Each to their own...

The lightest pocket notebook

If you don't want to weigh yourself down with a notebook, simply carry a sheet of paper. In Tokyo, you still see older people taking large pieces of paper from out of their pockets. They fold them four or eight times so they can fit in the palm. Every side represents one page of a small diary. This comes in very useful if you want to jot down your ideas while you're waiting for the bus, or scribble something down, like an entry code or a telephone number.

Where to keep your notebook

Your notebook should not only be your taskmaster. It should also be your constant companion. It transcends mere productivity; it curates your thoughts, desires and aspirations. It can be a portal into a magical, secret world. When you are at home, always keep your notebook close to hand. To help you sleep at night, keep it on your bedside table so you can write down the things you worry you'll forget to do the next day. In the morning, as soon as you wake up, write down your dreams. During the day, it will be useful in the kitchen (for your recipes), in the living room and on your desk.

Keep your notes up to date. When you do everything in good time, you can live fully in the present moment. Just try it. You will feel better than you ever have before. Keep everything you want to keep private in a safe place (in a case or trunk which locks).

2

How to write lists

How to begin

The most difficult thing at the outset is finding a way to organise your lists, and coming up with the chapter headings and section headings. Where do you begin your list of memories, your list of dreams… ? Simply start with where you are today. Your book of lists cannot be written in a matter of days or weeks. It will grow gradually, as a function of passing time, moods, rememberings and events.

You could start with the type of list which appeals to you most. Or with a recent event. For example, if you have just received a present, write at the top of a blank page 'Presents I have received'. Write down what you have been given and the date. Soon, all sorts of lists will follow. Have patience.

At the beginning you will make mistakes, in terms of how you order your lists and how you present them… but in these missteps you will find the style of presentation and expression which works best for you.

Different types of lists

READING NOTES

Why keep all the books you have read? Books will clutter your home. Ask yourself, how many of the books you've kept have you actually reread? Then ask yourself how many new books you want to read? Books not only attract dust, they also nibble away at the space we have, space we can't increase. Why not get rid of the books you probably won't reread – give them to friends, to libraries, charity shops, or sell them. Let other people take pleasure from these books. You can make notes on them and only keep your very dearest books, the ones you feel intimately connected with, your friends for life. Or the books you refer to often. Pass the other books on. Only keep your favourites.

LISTS ON DIFFERENT-COLOURED PAPER

Write on lined paper or write on coloured paper. Indulge your whims. Perhaps write lists of everyday things on pink paper, lists of 'pleasures of the mind' on grey paper (for grey matter), and so on. This allows you to easily identify different types of lists in your ring binder.

LISTS IN TWO COLUMNS

These are useful for questions which are pending, for facts and their interpretations (coincidences, perhaps) and for transcribing conversations. Date these so you know exactly when they happened.

LISTS AS WORKS OF ART

Consider making your lists more artistic; for example, with different colours, straight lines and curved lines, overlappings and shaded sections. By using words, shapes and colours, you can even create a mandala (a geometric rendering of the universe, which is used in meditation by some Asian religions). Explore the styles and methods which appeal to you. True artists can express themselves in mandalas interspersed with text.

One of my friends studied Baudelaire by shading each 'mood' in his poems with a different colour. The art of the list can be very creative. You can create a sequence of lists in different colours. You can, in some of your lists, accompany each entry with a small drawing. And if you are not good at drawing, this little daily exercise will help you improve.

CALLIGRAPHY LISTS

Learn to write beautifully using a fountain pen, or perhaps several fountain pens with different sizes of nib, or even with brushes. Copy out the poems and expressions which speak to you the most. This activity is both artistic and wonderfully relaxing.

LISTS IN THE SHAPE OF SNAKES, CIRCLES, PYRAMIDS, SYMBOLS

Take inspiration from poets and writers. Transcribe the words you love, or lists of mantras, in new and original ways. This guards against boredom.

LISTS AS PAINTINGS – OF LANDSCAPES, OF PEOPLE

Why not use watercolours to express your dreams?

EMBELLISHED LISTS

Why not go to a library and look at ancient books? Copy some of the flourishes used on letters to customise your own lists.

LISTS AS SKETCHES

Japan is a nation of gourmets. Many Japanese people, while travelling, use lists to sketch the meals they have eaten. They use arrows to come back to the names of the ingredients. They include the plates the meal is served on, their colour and shape. The presentation of the meal is every bit as important as the recipe. This sort of list is an excellent way of remembering all the component parts of a meal – both aesthetic and gastronomic. It is far more interesting than simply taking a photo on your phone.

'COLLAGE' LISTS

Stick a small photo of the author at the top of the page, along-side the title of the book you are making notes on. When you see a photo of an author you have read and written about, cut it out of the magazine or newspaper. If you are compiling your lists on a computer, cut and paste the photo from a website.

LISTS TO WRITE AS A COUPLE, AS A FAMILY OR AS A GROUP

Writing a 'portrait list' as a couple, describing the life and feelings you share, can be an excellent way of 'refreshing' your relationship (do not be afraid to write things which are less than flattering). This type of list can be written in a park, on a picnic blanket, around a campfire... Or you can, as a family, compose lists of memories. And everyone can ask questions about family members they never knew. The blood of our ancestors runs in our veins.

LISTS TO SHARE

Ask your mother or grandmother to write down the lyrics to the songs they sang in their youth, their cordon bleu recipes, their favourite quotes or poems. This can lead to more closeness, more exchange.

LISTS TO GIVE

Just imagine a list of your recipes or your favourite quotes, written on a pretty piece of paper and rolled up in a ribbon. This could be a very special gift for someone dear to you. It's just like the way teenagers give mixtapes of their favourite songs to their best friends and lovers…

NUMBERED LISTS

'Throughout human history, numbers have given shape to time, whether according to cosmic factors, or other factors. Numbers can stretch time, expand time, consolidate time and punctuate time. Numbers stretch to infinity. The list of "things" in The Pillow Book *by Sei Shonagon, or* The Exhaustion of Images *by Jacqueline Pigeot, the methods of enumeration… Twenty years after Shonagon, Tokugen came up with an art of the list which was even more complex. Broken down into sequences (for example, by colour), every list assembles similar elements. For example, the great variety of violet things: violet moorland, a violet dress, violet sandalwood, the violet chrysanthemums on Mount Kurai… violet recurs in many different spheres. But whether the list is homogenous or heterogeneous, whether linear or branching out in many directions, this sort of list is a peculiarly Japanese phenomenon, the* mono zukushi. *Yes, these lists do draw inspiration from Chinese sources (for example, the 41 lists of Li Shang-yin), and the lists made by Dutch botanists played a role in the development of drawn*

lists (for example, Manga by Hokusai). But in the particular case of Japanese lists, the key relation is between numbers and things. By numbering things, by putting them in a sequence, by multiplying them and adding them up, things are grouped, sometimes harmoniously and sometimes not. This makes us see things more intensely, as a function of small differences and gaps in meaning. By understanding the power of numbers, we come back to the paradigms of sacred immanence, which doesn't have single form, or indeed a trinity, but exists as a multiple. One thousand is a symbolic number, denoting a thousand human faces.'

Christine Buci-Glucksmann, *The Aesthetic of Time in Japan*

Numbers have a symbolic power. One thousand is infinity. Seven – as in the seven rings of the bell; three times seven, for the striking of the gong; the seven rocks in a Zen garden – is the number of Zen; it brings good luck. What differentiates lists from other ways of storing information – whether written, audio or visual – is the way the information must be organised, classified, selected and edited.

Some lists in numbers:

108 harmful things and desires we want to rid ourselves of, represented by the sound of the gong used to summon the divinities to help us in this quest

Lists of 1 (things which are unique)

Lists of 2 (things which complement each other, yin and yang)

Lists of 7

Lists of 10 (the Ten Commandments, and so on.)

Lists of X, X being my favourite number

Lists of 100

Lists of 1,000 (but categories which can come under this heading, as opposed to lists with 1,000 separate entries, e.g. My 1,000 pleasures, 1,000 thank yous, 1,000 kisses).

Give each of your lists a title

Every topic is like a border, a demarcation. Editing means eliminating everything which has no purpose, then rearranging what remains in a way which is logical, coherent and clear. In order to do that, everything which lies outside that system must be 'dealt with', and by that I mean deleted or moved elsewhere, so it doesn't blur the clear vision which is essential to the order of the list. Beauty and clarity will follow. But the most important thing of all is to give each of your lists a precise title. This will allow you to know exactly where to put your notes.

Once again, the key to a good collection of lists lies in the concision with which you demarcate the content. Here are some examples of potential titles:

Under Culture:
Books
Films
Exhibitions.

Under Travel:
Places I have visited
The names of hotels
Anecdotes
What I felt.

Under The Irrational World:

What I dream

Dreams for the future

My craziest dreams

Coincidences.

Under Information:

Things my friends have recommended to me

Useful phone numbers.

Under IT:

Internet sites

Passwords

Keyboard shortcuts.

When to write lists

*'One's diary is a place where one doesn't
have to worry about being perfect.'*

Anaïs Nin

When Anaïs Nin wrote her journal, she had the habit of sitting quietly
for a few minutes before starting to write. She would close her eyes
and allow herself to go back over the most significant events of her
day, and the things which provoked the strongest feelings.

As I've said, making lists is a way of writing a diary, albeit in a
very minimalistic form. Making lists shows a fierce determination
to understand life and to give it meaning. Making lists is a way of
trying to put your life in order, of finding the logic in it. But writing
needn't take up more space in your life than you'd like it to: lists give
us the freedom to write whenever we want, wherever we are and,
above all, whenever the fancy takes us.

For example:

In a café, in a traffic jam, scribble down some ideas of playlists
you would like to compile.

When you're eating a sandwich, write down twenty things
you'd like to do before you die.

During the commercials on television, write down what you
have just listened to, or what you would like to do during the
holidays.

In the doctor's waiting room, jot down ten things you could do
to live more healthily.

Every evening write a dozen entries, like a memory or two from childhood, a dish which you would like to cook. In a year, you will have 4,380 entries, in ten years 43,800 – a veritable treasure trove.

3

Books of lists which may inspire you

Jonathan's lists

Jonathan, a friend of mine from New York, once wrote me a list of the lists he has lost:

'Dominique gave me the idea that a list can reveal a lot about a person. So I began to compile a list: a list of ten lists I'd really cherished but which are now lost. A list of lost lists. Here it is:

1. A list of the names of the cats at Casa Azul in Mexico, where Frida Kahlo once lived, written in a notebook in 1995. I'd noticed a lot of cats there, and asked the gardener for their names. I wrote them down carefully. Obviously there was ultimately no point.
2. An illustrated list of African batik fabrics I had made in a school jotter when staying in Accra, Ghana in 1990. A rare visual project.

3. A list of the vinyls I owned, saved on a 5¼-inch disk, on a first-generation IBM PC. The last time I consulted it was 1987.

4. The names of the people who attended an unforgettable evening at Samassekolu, in Accra's Russian district, in October 1990. The guests came from so many different countries and spoke so many different languages. If I remember correctly, we must have used at least twenty different languages that evening: Hausa, Bambara, English, Akan...

5. A list, in a jotter, of all the meals I ate with my friend Elizabeth between 1995 and 1997. The jotter disappeared mysteriously on a bus in 1997. We started again from scratch but this new jotter, which I still have, doesn't contain much.

6. A list of songs by Straight Edge, a band I played bass in, in the form of a table of electronic data. I left it with the band when I quit in 1996.

7. A list of the classics I read following a 1986 performance of *Samson*, the oratorio by Handel. The first book on the list was *Paradise Lost* by John Milton. I lost this list in 1988.

8. Lists of pieces of jazz music I listened to on WKCR radio between 1988 and 1989, each one dated and sorted by the name of the artist and album. A great resource to examine my musical tastes and how they evolved in those years.

9. A list of the cycle rides I made in July 1988 in Brooklyn – I cycled more than 1,600 km. I always ask myself how many

times I'd have had to cycle round Central Park or Prospect Park to reach this figure.

10. A list of letters I wrote on a typewriter during a stay in Africa. They are all dated and sorted by the recipient and the subject. For me these are a treasure, and I really must get them back. Sometimes I say to myself that, in the intervening decades, I have written about the same things, gone back over the same ground, in all my correspondence. It would be a great pleasure to reread those letters.

The Great Almanac of Japanese Poetry

This work is perhaps the most important anthology in the history of Japanese literature.

It is a very detailed collection of dates and memorial traditions, and a repertoire of the characteristics of the seasons, with poems paying tribute to each of those seasons. This collection lies at the heart of Japanese culture.

It contains more than 4,900 expressions, evoking the different seasons and everything relating to them (in terms of clothes, the life cycles of plants and animals, food…) Everyone could draw from this book their own inspirations in terms of phrases to put into verse.

Each of the five almanacs (one for each of the seasons, and one for the new year) is divided into seven parts:

1. The seasons
2. The sky and its moods
3. Rivers and mountains
4. Human life
5. Festivals and ceremonies
6. Monsters
7. What plants say.

The *Dao de jing* by Lao-tseu

This book, which is considered the bible of Taoism, is a treaty composed of sentences relating to 'the principle and its corresponding action'. Containing observations on nature on 'the empty and the mute', this small book is a long list of simple principles (simple in appearance only) to understand, and to apply to yourself, as you would like others to apply them to themselves.

This is another book to 'assimilate' into your life, to make it richer and more profound.

Notes by Li Yi-chan

The lists of Li Yi-chan, an eighth-century Chinese poet, were directories of sorts. They are mirrors on the world, suggesting, for example, the richness or poverty of the era by listing the meals eaten, the means of heating, and so on.

> *'Whispers of reading, the laziness that implies, liquors and teas, which at the time were as rare as they were expensive.'*

Yi-chan packaged up his lists with the intention of returning to his native country to see out his final days. But he died three days before he reached Chinese shores.

He was said never to have written without first consulting a number of reference books, and for that reason had been given the surname T'a Su Yu, which means otter. In China, the otter is thought to place its catch on the riverbank and contemplate it before beginning to eat.

The same author gave us the *tsa-ts'ouan*, marvellous 'directory lists', which inspired Sei Shonagon and Urabe Kenko in Japan. These lists were written on strips of paper tied together with string, which can still be found in shops selling calligraphy materials in Japan. Sei Shonagon used these as pillows (traditionally, a Japanese pillow would be a little wooden stand, designed to keep the shape of the courtesan's hair, and which would sometimes also contain a secret casket). Hence the title *The Pillow Book*.

A few extracts from the forty-two lists which make up the
tsa-ts'ouan:

> Things which do not go together (for example, a butcher and a
> Buddhist text)
>
> People who dare not show their faces in public because of
> shame (for example, the pregnant nun)
>
> People who are scared of being found out (for example, the
> adulterer)
>
> Things we do not hate (for example, finding shelter after a long
> walk)
>
> People who are not in a hurry (for example, the young wife
> receiving visitors)
>
> Resemblances (for example, swallows and nuns; both are
> always with a companion)
>
> Things it is better not to know (for example, alcohol, for the
> monk)
>
> Annoying things (for example, not being able to eat certain
> foods when you have an upset stomach).

Sages écrits de jadis

Sages écrits de jadis is a collection of different maxims in the form of quotes, poems, aphorisms and popular sayings (like the Japanese, the Chinese seek harmony, within families and in the wider social life). This anthology contains a vast array of different authors, philosophies and styles. The content is diverse, rich and restrained in equal measure. This creates a certain harmony between sources as varied as the classics of Chinese antiquity and the famous novels of Yuan and Ming. This genre of short texts is a common one in China.

Many themes are explored in this small book. The Chinese like talking in proverbs, and what a pleasure it is to read and reread this selection of the best.

The editor of the compilation, Dan Yang, explains:

'A lot of the maxims recommend cultivating the virtues of patience and self-mastery. Every entry in this book can touch you to the very core and enlighten every moment of your existence. This is the appeal of maxims for people who are in search of wisdom. After all, the end goal of all human knowledge is to know how to retain your humanity and enjoy the best life has to offer.'

Here are some examples from the book:

> 'If you do only good deeds you will have nothing to worry about in the future.'

> 'Hold your tongue as you would stopper a bottle; defend yourself against desires in the same way you would defend a city.'

'Prefer to be wronged than to wrong others.'

'Only say two or three words to people you meet. It would not be prudent to confide everything.'

'If you are weak, do not take on heavy burdens.'

'Be humble, do not give advice.'

'Friendship is as fragile as a sheet of paper.'

'The outcome of life can change as quickly as the outcome of a game of chess.'

'If you want to stop drinking, look at drunks.'

'Contain the anger of the moment and avoid one hundred days of bother.'

Conclusion

'Every man is a link in a chain. He gives a form to existence, to his own existence, or rather he should do. Otherwise he will be a seed destined to rot in the ground, having failed to generate his own development. In this way, we are all obliged to let our lives play out, and to act. There are no inferior beings, only beings who do not want to rise up, to develop the growth programmed in their very beings.'

Théodore Monod

Life is, and remains, one breath after another, one thought at a time, one world leading to another. Create your own reality by creating a chain of little lists. That way, you will not only make sure life doesn't slip through your fingers, but you will seize it, savour it and live it better.

And, more than anything, remember...
The key word is WRITE.

THESE PAGES ARE FOR YOUR OWN NOTES

Take pleasure in keeping a list of affirmations, challenges, advice, needs and circumstances. These words will be a comfort to carry with you whenever you need them.

L'art de la
SIMPLICITÉ
HOW TO LIVE MORE WITH LESS

Dominique Loreau

To simplify your life is to enrich it. Discover the magic of simplicity in this international bestseller.